A Philosophy of Mindfulness

A Journey with Deleuze

FINN JANNING

NFB
Buffalo, New York
USA

Printed in The United States of America
ISBN: 978-0-9984018-8-1

A Philosophy of Mindfulness: A Journey with Deleuze /
Janning-1st ed.

1. Philosophy. 2. Mindfulness. 3. Deleuze.
4. Meditation. 5. Buddhism. 6. Janning.

NFB/Amelia Press
<<<>>>
119 Dorchester Road
Buffalo, New York 14213 USA
For more information please visit
nfbpublishing.com

For Griselda, Askild, Hjalte, and Smilla—con amor.

I wrote my book to free myself from it,
not to be its prisoner.

– Elena Ferrante, *Frantumaglia*

CONTENTS

Preface

SOME YEARS AGO, I WAS TEACHING A COURSE IN PHILO-sophical Counseling. To my surprise, all that the students wanted to know was "What is the right thing to do?" Having that knowledge, they assumed, would make life easier. "Perhaps," I said, "but not better or more interesting."

Their request is part of the obsessive achievement eagerness of today's society to perform well according to fixed ideals. It creates dullness when it comes to mental exercises. The unfortunate norm is the faster the better. I told them that philosophy is about developing problems, not delivering solutions. It's a slow practice. It's for life. My answer made them fidget with impatience. To philosophize, I emphasized, is to dwell on the fundamental questions, and these questions are developed in problems, just as the problems are enveloped in fundamental questions.

Yet, my students insisted: "So, what is the right question?"

I told them that this particular question was related

to the problem embedded in the question. For example, how do you draw a clear distinction between right and wrong?

The ones who weren't paying attention looked up from their screens.

In sports, where the rules are given, I said, it is rather obvious to tell whether a player is "doing it wrong." Similarly, in business, where profit seems to guide every decision, knowing what is right and wrong may be easier. Life, however, is neither a game nor a business, although there is a tendency to classify people into winners and losers as if life were that simple. Such labeling is a part of today's achievement society. Everyone's performance is measured according to an ideal—an ideal that is often related to the status, prestige, power, and, of course, money that is associated with being a winner.

They were silent, so I went on. Of course, there are things in life that are rather obvious. For instance, no one needs philosophy to tell you that it is wrong to kill, discriminate against, or repress other people. Instead, philosophy begins when we start questioning the obvious. Could I live another life? What is also possible? How may I also live?

A part of philosophy is to accept that some problems remain without a solution; some questions can't be answered once and for all.

Such a question is *Which life is worth living?*

Of course, one of my students then asked me: "Which life is worth living?"

This is how this book begins.

* * * *

This book circles around three ideas. First, I try to answer the question "Which life is worth living?" through the application of the French philosopher Gilles Deleuze's affirmative philosophy. Second, I claim that we need a "new" philosophy because we— many of us, at least—are blind. We see rather little of that which surrounds us. This claim leads to the third idea, which is perhaps the most complicated: I relate Deleuze's philosophy to mindfulness. Hereby, I don't wish to suggest that they are identical. They are not. The differences are essential. Yet, mixing mindfulness with Deleuze leads to a philosophy of mindfulness, one that makes us less blind but also ethically responsible in relation to what we experience. Thus, I move mindfulness from the sphere of psychology into philosophy, or from being primarily an inward-turned practice to an outward-turned one.

A philosophy of mindfulness puts emphasis on experience, experiment, and actualization or affirmation. Each experience matters; life is the experience of making contact or being connected with what is in the midst of becoming—that is, life—and then passing it on to the next generations.

WHICH LIFE IS WORTH LIVING?

1

It begins with a paradox. All "of Deleuze's work is concerned with ethics, in that ethical principles inform his basic conception of thought and what it means to think."[1] Still, "Deleuze is not ordinarily the first to come to mind when one considers continental philosophers who have made significant contributions to ethical thought."[2]

One of the reasons why the French thinker doesn't come to mind when we are dealing with ethical issues could be that he is unknown. This may be the case outside of a philosophical context; however, within the world of philosophy, he is regarded as one of the most important and original voices emerging from the 20th century. More likely, the reason for his absence is due to the way in which we think. Many people understand ethics as something more or less similar to morals: a set of baseline values and norms that are rarely questioned.

Ethics is not moralism. It is an explorative way of living. As Michel Foucault said in the preface to Deleuze and Guattari's *Anti-Oedipus*, "I would say that Anti-Oedipus (may its authors forgive me) is a book of *ethics* . . . being anti-oedipal has become a life style, a way of thinking and living."[3]

Ethics is a way of thinking and living—a lifestyle. In other words, if we live rather miserably, it must be because we think like that; or if our thinking is too naive or banal, it is because we live like that. Linking living, thinking, and acting make this ethic therapeutic in the sense that it makes us see things, such as new possibilities and forms of life, which we may not otherwise have seen. It presents us with alternative forms of life. If I can think differently, I can also live differently. In thinking begins living; in living begins thinking. The term therapeutic—philosophically— does not refer to a process of *normalizing*, for example, seeing your past in a different shade. Rather, it is to make everything more real—not to explain, but to enhance, enlarge, and unfold.

Two of Deleuze's philosophical admirers—Nietzsche and Spinoza—are also therapeutic in an ethical sense. Nietzsche, for example, spoke about the "philosopher physician," who had the courage to say that philosophy is not about truth, but rather health, power, and life, whereas Spinoza claimed that philosophy is a practice of wisdom.

Philosophical wisdom, therefore, is neither something given nor a fixed identity; rather, it is related to becoming mature. For example, an immature person may not pay to ride the subway, thereby undermining the future existence of what they themselves are using; it is as if the person is sawing off the branch that he or she sits on.

A tentative answer to which life is worth living is a mature life . . . a life that knows that he or she is intimately linked to other forms of life—organic as well as inorganic. Philosophy as "a way of thinking and living," therefore, is not only oriented toward life but also integrates into and eventually *becomes* life. It's "the art of living. It is a concrete attitude and determinate lifestyle, which engages the whole existence."[4]

In ancient Greece in 5th century B.C., the idea of freedom was born that gradually led to a therapy for life. All things were to be examined and called into question. The approaches varied, yet all philosophers at that time were concerned with how we may excel in living. There were no limits set on what to think and how to live. It stresses that philosophy is more than an armchair exercise; it releases pain and suffering, and it makes life more bearable not by explaining but through exploration. In this sense, philosophy is always personal but also selfless. It deals with life. Therefore, you go where life takes you, not where some idea suggests that you should go. In a letter to his friend, the philosopher Ludwig Wittgenstein wrote, "What is the use of studying philosophy if all it does for you is to enable you to talk with some plausibility about some abstruse questions in logic, etc. & if it does not improve your thinking about the important questions of everyday life, if it does not make you more conscientious."[5]

In continuation hereof, I ask rhetorically: What is more important than life? What could be of greater interest than knowing which life is worth living, not just for yourself, your children, or friends, but for everyone?

* * * *

Thinking is an engagement with life. It vibrates in between what is *no longer* and *not yet*. Three questions seem to be implicitly present: How do you *experience* the present living moment? How do you *experiment* with the present living moment? How do you *actualize* what is unknown—but nevertheless real—in the present living moment? Experience moves us from being passive to active. To affirm is to be accountable for what you bring to life.

Living these three questions, I propose, leads to a life worth living. What answers the questions may produce, I don't know. We all have to battle with life alone, but luckily always with a little help from family, friends, philosophers, meditators, or whoever may touch us in a useful way.

To illustrate this process, I will relate Deleuze's thinking to meditation, mainly mindfulness. Mindfulness is a fundamental aspect of Buddhist practice. Several definitions are as follows: "Mindfulness means paying attention in a particular way: on purpose, in the present moment, and nonjudgmentally." "Mindfulness is about being fully aware of what is happening in the present moment, without filters or the lens of judgment." "Mindfulness is simply observing, watching, examining. You are not a judge but a scientist."[6]

Some constant concepts are *being fully aware, the present moment, nonjudgmentally,* and *memory of the present moment.* Keeping the present in mind is the opposite of forgetfulness.

I refer to mindfulness for two reasons: (1) it can help to establish the condition in which we experience what is happening (i.e., make us less blind), and (2) yet, it stops (conditioning our experience) where Deleuze's affirmative and creative philosophy begins.

In other words, mindfulness deals with the first two of my three questions: How do you *experience* the present living moment? How do you *experiment* with the present living moment?

The kind of life that is worth living fully experiences what takes place. However, it also experiments and examines life in order to develop the best possible path. Linking Deleuze's ethical philosophy with mindfulness, I believe, gives it a more "operational" touch. Mindfulness can help people pay attention, which is part of an affirmative philosophy. Simone Weil describes attention as something, "which is so full that the 'I' disappears."[7] "I" becomes someone else.

As I will gradually show, attention then turns into becoming. However, this only occurs *if* you are capable of letting go of the idea of having a permanent and unchangeable self or "I," and if you stop clinging to your previous or current faculty of knowledge. You become through exposure. Here, philosophy resembles writing. "We write only at the frontiers of our knowledge, at the border which separates our knowledge from our ignorance and transforms the one into the other."[8]

It is by acknowledging and questioning our ignorance that we learn. I hope that this book will leave readers with more questions than answers since the art of living is related to the art of questioning. A life worth living takes nothing for granted but is open and curious regarding everything. It moves from nowhere to everywhere.

* * * *

"We really do lack in general a particle of the East, a grain of Zen," Deleuze says as he tries to sketch a philosophy that is "one-third Zen."⁹ I propose one-third mindfulness.

A one-third mindfulness philosophy is like a refreshing breeze or wind. Thinking is like encountering a caressing breath of fresh air. The Latin word "spiritus" means "breath," as well as "spirit" or "soul." However, the spirituality associated with Deleuze's philosophy is not, as it is often understood nowadays, an individual quest for the meaning of life or soul searching. A philosophy of mindfulness is, on the contrary, a way of overcoming individuality. All identity markers are forms of imprisonment that hinder a direct and spontaneous contact with life. So, instead of operating with a higher spirit (i.e., deity), I propose that spirituality can also be understood as a liberating breeze that connects . . . a breath, which unfortunately is often kept in a hermetic box that makes us suffocate. Therefore, a philosophy of mindfulness believes that there is something larger and greater than me, which is life. But life is here. There was life before me, and a part of my purpose here is to pass on life to future generations.

Although meditation is mostly associated with the Buddhist tradition, the term has a long tradition within philosophy—for example, Marcus Aurelius' *Meditations* or Descartes' *Meditations*—just as meditation is found in all the big religions, including Christianity, Islam, and Hinduism, as well as shamanism. Sometimes, the word is connected with contemplation and vice versa. According to *Thesaurus.com,* contemplation means not just religious or ideological reflection but also thoughtful observation, deep consideration, purpose, or intention. It's the latter descriptions I aim at here. In old French, *meditacion* is "thought, reflection, study"; in Latin, *meditationem* refers to "thinking over, meditation." Interestingly, it also refers to "to measure, limit, consider, advise, take appropriate measures," which provides useful associations with the middle way, balance, and harmony concepts that are often used in ethical writings. Last, the word also has roots in the Greek *mederi* ("to heal") and *medicus* ("physician"). Mindfulness, for example, is regarded as healing. "While it may not be possible for us to cure ourselves or to find someone who can, it is possible for us to *heal* ourselves— to learn to live with and work with the conditions that present themselves in the present moment . . . Healing is a transformation of view rather than cure . . . Above all, it involves learning to feel at home and at peace within yourself."[10]

Regardless of the associations that spirituality and meditations awaken, I don't assume or propose that spiritual refers to something holy; however, meditation can help you endure difficult moments in your life. There is also a clear line between philosophy and religion. That is, between "philosophy's love of immanence and religion's devotion to transcendence or 'vertical Being' . . . Deleuze, then, is a thinker of the infinite: of infinite movement and of infinite speed precisely because he is a thinker of immanence."[11]

For example, mindfulness is said to "be the remembering of the objects of mind and the senses received at the sense-door—of which the mind is considered the sixth. It is said to have the characteristic of 'being present in.'"[12] Here, the key concept is "being present in" and how to understand this. If "being present in" alludes to the idea that the present moment is something that you can step in and out of, then it is problematic. The present moment is not a swimming pool with a clear border. You are still present whether you are aware of it or not. Therefore, what mindfulness wishes to stress is that thinking *about* what happens takes you *out* of the present moment. It also stresses that everything moves from this present moment, so that time folds around itself, while everything passes through in each present moment. Technically, we can't escape that time is in us, even though many apparently try (e.g., cosmetic surgery). It is time that changes us.

Paying attention to each moment, therefore, is mandatory, but without turning the present moment into a holy grail or an object that only leads to attachment. Each moment is just the previous one being dissolved into the present, which again is being dissolved into the next. We are constantly producing the past while keeping the future open. In mindfulness, however, the "present moment" often represents something sacred. It presents us with a horizon, the limits of reality; yet, the aim of philosophy is to undo such structure. Life can't be framed without being inhibited.

In continuation, Deleuze is a strictly immanent and atheistic philosopher. This has been a coherent element in his thinking. In *Nietzsche and Philosophy,* published in 1962, he wrote: "Pluralism is the properly philosophical way of thinking, the one principle of a violent atheism."[13] Believing that all authority comes from God is to resign from thinking. More than twenty years later, in an interview in 1989, he said, "Religions are worth much less than the nobility and the courage of the atheisms which they inspire."[14]

The risk of having faith in a higher order is that it

makes us less receptive and creative regarding what happens with us. Philosophy and religion are like water and oil. "Whenever there is transcendence, vertical Being, imperial State in the sky or on the earth, there is religion; and there is Philosophy whenever there is immanence, even if it functions as arena for the agon and rivalry."[15]

Religion is normally understood as something that binds or unites the human being together and with the world by referring to norms of human behavior that are guaranteed by a superhuman authority. Such authority can manifest itself in two manners—either as a supernatural deity or through natural laws. Although science is based on natural laws, it's not a religion (although some may treat science this way). Science discovers and describes how things function; yet, it doesn't prescribe a universal set of moral rules and behaviors. Instead, science proposes theories to explain what is happening, which can then be tested, verified, nuanced, or falsified. It's a zigzagging process, not necessarily a linear progression, which some scientists tend to forget. Similarly, a game of chess is not religion, although it consists of certain rules that regulate the movement of each piece. The rules of chess are defined or invented by humans (and, therefore, they could change). Religion makes sense through an ultimate referent: god or nature that can't be proved. Nevertheless, religion can offer a narrative framework that may reduce our pain, suffering, doubts, and anxieties in life. It can add meaning to what seems meaningless. Examples are the stories about what happens in the afterlife. Thus, fear of punishment or a general anxiety for the unknown can make it tempting for some to lean onto the seductive religious stories. Regardless of what religion has to offer, I would like to emphasize two things against a religious framework. First, religion minimizes or eliminates our pains, fear, and anxiety, which also eliminates our doubts and ignorance—the fuel of knowledge production. It may hinder us from becoming wiser and more mature. Second, operating with an ultimate referent, as well as a final objective and how to get there (e.g., rules and norms), makes us less free, less innovative, and less creative. Perhaps for this reason, Deleuze and Guattari write: "It is amazing that so many philosophers still take the death of God as tragic. Atheism is not a drama but the philosopher's serenity and philosophy's achievement."[16]

Abandoning religion doesn't lead to nihilism or disbelief. On the contrary, a philosophy of mindfulness has faith in life. Yet, life is difference, and what happens in between life and death doesn't and shouldn't follow one way. What I advocate for is philosophy where critical and affirmative thinking coheres. Saying yes to life is, at the same time, saying no to what destroys it.

* * * *

Philosophy, as it is presented here, is the art of living, where living is a creative and experimenting practice. The unexamined life is not worth living, Socrates said. The difference, therefore, between a mindful and affirmative philosophy and then, for example, Plato is one of examination. It's one of style. That is, how we examine.

To think is to create, which requires that we are mindful of how we intermingle and become *with* life.

Nothing is given for certain, whether in the past, present, or future.

2

BEING MINDFUL IS PART OF THE ROLE OF THE ARTIST, "The artist is a seer, a becomer."[17] The artist has seen something—something that he or she passes on in a way that gives the reader enhanced access to this world. For instance, a novel is a communication of experiences that typically involves ethics and knowledge. A novel answers the questions of how a person acts, reflects, thinks, and feels during certain circumstances. This is why literature can be a way of gaining experiences that make us more mature by allowing us to experience other forms of life. The artist is a seer, and he or she confronts the reader with his or her ethical limitations.

"In the act of writing there's an attempt to make life something more than personal, to free life from what imprisons it . . . You write with a view to an unborn people that doesn't yet have a language. Creating isn't communicating but resisting."[18] Writing is resisting following the dominating fantasies and ideas controlling our lives. It is avoiding using the same template: Arh, it must be because of your father or mother. You write to give the unborn a possibility to live free—that is, to live a healthy life. "The ultimate aim of literature is to set free, in the delirium, this creation of a health or this invention of a people, that is, a possibility of life. To write for this people who are missing . . . ('for' means less 'in the place of' than 'for the benefit of')."[19]

The writer is affirming. "*To affirm is not to take responsibility for, to take on the burden of what is, but to release, to set free what lives.* To affirm is to unburden, not to load life with the weight of higher values, but *to create* new values which are those of life, which make life light and active."[20] To release, set free, and create values of life . . . this is why we want to spend time with certain writers; they extend our boundaries.

The writer is generous when he or she passes on life. This also indicates that to produce art (or think philosophically), there has to be something at stake: it's a matter of life and death. "A creator who isn't grabbed around the throat by a set of impossibilities is no creator."[21]

Referring to Primo Levi's suicide, Deleuze says in *L'Abécédaire de Gilles Deleuze*, "He committed suicide personally . . . Ah yes, ah yes, he could no longer hold on, so he committed suicide to his personal life. Bet, there are four pages or twelve pages or a hundred pages of Primo Levi that will remain, that will remain eternal resistances."

Both art and philosophy are practices that affirm life. The artist resembles Nietzsche's Übermench, "the overman," who can affect the lives of others via his or her creation of values. The values produced through a certain form of life transgress the set of values and norms that the masses uncritically take as given—that is, without really reflecting on where the values come from, what the values of these values are, etc. The masses represent a generic and mediocre form of life, as Ortega y Gasset said in *La Rebellion de las Masas*, where "being different is indecent."[22] The values produced by the Übermench are open to alternative ways of living. Here, it is not only indecent not to be different but also restrictive since everyone is different.

Art, like philosophy, is impersonal. In other words, the artist who only passes on his or her personal story, for example, saying, "Look how I've suffered," "I've been around the world," "I've seen it all," is guided by vanity (or narcissism), and not by freeing life. Similarly, the artist who condemns without producing an alternative is, at most, only moralizing. Art that doesn't explore or scrutinize what it means to be a human today isn't art.

* * * *

The *art* of living a life worth living is referring to art as in the *artist*. Art is not moralizing or representing, but pushing our sensibility further, making us more sensible (i.e., ethical). Art, for this same reason, is the only thing that can resist death. Homer, Don Quixote, and Mona Lisa's smile are still with us today. Art is always contemporary.

Let me give an example. In 2008, I am at Fundazione Nicola Trusszandi in Milan, walking around paintings and sculptures from the last two hundred years, but then something happens. I encounter the German artist Tino Sehgal's "live pieces" or happenings. I propose the term "live pieces" because Sehgal does not document his work and what happens seems random at first, but later it is obvious that it is not. As I walk around the museum, four attendants suddenly jump into the room as if jumping out of the wall while singing, "This is contemporary." Their words stress that this actually happens at the same time as the rest of the museum's work—a historical span of more than 200 years is present—here and now. The past is folded into the present, just as the present unfolds a coming future. However, I don't really experience it. Not yet. Not until they awaken me. In another room is a very intimate young couple. I leave them. Then, I pass a woman lying on the floor. Is she suffering or ecstatic? Should I do something? Before resolving what to do, an attendant starts stripping in front of me. She takes off her clothes. Slowly. A few people arrive, and then they move on, not sure whether she is stripping for me only. Another couple passes; they stop for a while, and then they move on as well. I can't move on. Her nakedness is different from the numerous paintings of naked women. The live stripping illustrates how the female body is a source of power and subjection. She may be the subject of my attention, but I am subjected to her moves. None of this is random. There are no coincidences. Rather, Sehgal's live pieces show that we often look for explanations elsewhere when we can't grasp the moment. I stop analyzing. At last, I am just grounded right there in front of her. My thoughts don't wander. Not even when she gets up and gathers her clothes and leaves. I am still there. *What happened?* As I pass the rest of the exhibition, I notice how Sehgal's interventions have strengthened my attention; now, I really see the paintings on the wall and the sculptures that I pass. Why is it only children and women who are naked? I experience differently, more alert, more curious. I notice how the role of the flesh, the gender, the body has changed. I am placed between the past and the future.

* * * *

Why do I dwell so much on the artist? Because art and philosophy are both practices that share something crucial: they see. Seeing means making contact with what happens . . . being connected with life. Seeing is also related to our capacity to be affected, which is crucial for not only experiencing, but also for experimenting and transforming—that is, creating alternative ways of living, feeling, and thinking.

It is here that mindfulness meditation can help make people, in general, become more in contact with their senses and aware. Hereby, I don't wish to claim that we can all become artists or philosophers—of course not. It's not the artist, or art, or even philosophy as such that matters, but how the artist and philosopher are affected and affect life. They see. That's interesting. Thus, it is my assumption or thesis that before we can even begin to experiment, perhaps even transform or create alternative ways of living and thinking, we have to be capable of seeing the state of reality. Therefore, what I aim for is mindfulness as an internal motor of exploring life, not a practice inspired by an external finality (as in Buddhism). Once we begin paying attention, then we also begin questioning—this is what I propose.

Far too many are not seeing sufficiently; instead, they live rather generically and uncritically towards what takes place in today's obsessed achievement society. Many do not allow being touched; they do not question. And if there is a critique, it is typically raised as a kind of paternal moralism (e.g., we *have* to or *ought* to do better in the way we treat x). Such critique is without any transformational or sustainable power because it overcomes one ideal—for example, consumerism—with another ideal—for example, simple living. The problem with the moral markers— should, have, ought, etc.—is not that they suggest that we can, rather, they tend to suggest that we can't do better than what the norm or ideal propose. For the same reason, moralizing is an ongoing battle between positioning oneself in opposition to something defined as being bad— saying "See how good I am," or worse, using others' bad behavior to glorify one's own actions.

An affirmative and mindful philosophy, contrastingly, is pre-positional; it aims at being worthy of the present living moment—that is, to experience it fully. Being worthy is also a creative act that resists ordering, structuring, or categorizing; instead, it unfolds. For example, art opens a new territory through notions such as sensation, encounter, minor, affect, virtual, and becomings. Art reveals the general state of our receptivity and sensibility. It shows the conditions of experience. It challenges us. How do you go on from here?

A simple example can illustrate this. Christopher Nolan's film *Interstellar* (2015) tells the story of a world with food shortages that forces the human species to find another home somewhere in the galaxy. This context opens for problematizing questions regarding what a home is, how each generation is responsible for the next, and whether we as human beings can see beyond our personal desires and wants, and think on behalf of the entire species or life as such. It also addresses the limits of sciences and the power of love as passing on what you can never have—that is, certainty of the future. Love, therefore, becomes more than Hollywood sweetness; rather, it stresses the impersonal nature of the encounter. Love changes us because "relations are always external to their terms."[23] In this particular film, the relationship between the daughter and the father is literally actualizing the virtual. The virtual is real but not yet actualized. For example, both the father's and the daughter's pasts and memories are virtualities that may become actualized in the present. The process of actualization, therefore, also becomes an editing of the past.

The father, who is a former astronaut, leaves his daughter when she is ten years old and returns when she is dying in her eighties after many years travelling in space looking for a home for "the people to come." As the father says, "It's like we've forgotten who we are—explorers, pioneers, not caretakers."

The concept "the people to come" does not refer to a specific class; it is not political but ethical. Rather, it refers to those forms of life, those modes of existence, for which there is no room today . . . those forms of life that are being neglected, silenced, or ignored. "Becoming is always double, and it is the double becoming that constitute the people to come and the new earth."[24] Becoming is liberation, even from our own home when this is hindering us to live. The film illustrates how the space—in the film, obviously, depicted by space travel—is active, intense, productive, and fruitful. It illustrates how the desire of the daughter and father moves from being one of lack and repression toward desire as something productive in the capacity of actualizing new ways of relating or connecting. They experience, experiment, and actualize in order to become someone else. Becomings, therefore, are impersonal just like love. It is never about "me" becoming something specific, but becoming imperceptible—that is, becoming *with* life.

Interstellar emphasizes how an encounter with life affects us, how we become minor while actualizing what is there but nevertheless repressed or silent (e.g., a more intuitive approach to life, less scientifically validated), how the virtual capacity of an encounter—that is, its capacity to affect us—depends on our sensibility . . . our capacity to be affected. Despite a grand distance in time and space, the father and daughter connect.

* * * *

To begin with, we need to see well. In other words, we need to polish our lenses so that we see the world as it actually is—not just what we expect or hope it to be. We need to free our interaction and involvement with life from all kind of imprisonments—expectations or ideologies—because this colors our perception. Similarly, our learning (or what we are being told) shapes our perception. We become our experiences. In the novel *The Blazing World*, Siri Hustvedt describes how a female artist, Harriet Burden, wants to be seen and recognized as an artist, not just as a wife. However, this recognition is difficult because the art world is a man's world; therefore, the sad moral is when you see a woman, you don't expect to see art. Life is being repressed. By changing her artistic name to Harry, she gradually experiences responses that are not limited by her gender. Still, the point is not that artistic women should use pseudonyms; rather, that we all should consciously or mindfully pay attention to how we perceive gender, age, race, and sexuality. That is confronting our potential blind spots.

Thus, going back to my initial question—"Which life is worth living?"—the answer is the one that sets free what lives. Such a road, path, or way, however, seldom exists beforehand; instead, it requires our engagement in the present living moment to actualize or construct them. A philosophy of mindfulness is an interrogation with life, which again becomes a critical view of how we see and understand the world.

Freedom is a prerequisite for living the good life. The problem with freedom is that we are *not* born free, as many assume. Rather, it is something we become. Freedom is related to the practice of wisdom, which is related to the art of living open and curiously toward what takes place.

How do we experience, experiment, and actualize such a life?

THREE PREMISES

3

The Metaphysics of Deleuze's Thought

IN NOVEMBER 1981, DELEUZE MADE THE FOLLOW-
ing announcement in an interview: "I feel I am a
pure metaphysician . . . when Bergson says that modern
science has not found its metaphysics, the metaphysics it
needs. It is this metaphysics that interests me."[25]

This remark, I believe, is a formidable invitation to
an affirmative philosophy.

Metaphysics literally means what is "beyond" or "be-
sides" (Greek *meta*) physics. Traditionally, metaphysics
aims at establishing an unshakable foundation that can
secure order. In this sense, it can be seen as the whole ar-
chitecture or design that holds reality together, for instance, through myths, religion, or scientific dogmas.

Yet, the aim is not to overcome this world; on the
contrary, we need to enhance our belief in this world.

How can we live, think, and experience life fully

without being limited? First, we can cultivate our sensibility and avoid a rigid faith in something beyond. Both can be achieved by suggesting a *metaphysic of becoming* contrary to one of being. Metaphysical questions are not scientifically testable; however, they may be seen as an underlying premise or postulate for a research program or approach to life. Hopefully, it will become clearer, as I move forward, why I emphasize this metaphysical point. It affects how we can think about freedom and life. To put it differently, a metaphysic of being is mainly what causes all the troubles, whether political, religious, or existential, when we organize societies, our spirituality, or lives in general in a way that assures identification with something desirable. It is such ideologies that Deleuze tends to make infunctional, illustrating how empty they are. "There is no other truth than the creation of the New," he says.[26] "New" should not be associated with marketing, such as the excitement of a new iPhone; rather, truth is related to the new when something appears that changes how we perceive the world. When I heard The Doors for the first time, for a moment I had to sit down. I needed to revise everything I knew about music at that time in my life. The "new" is a shock; it opens territories that before you didn't know existed. Similarly, when I encountered Andy Warhol's work and read Junot Diaz's *The Brief Wondrous Life of*

Oscar Wao, I experienced a new way of writing in between settled languages. Such experiences can happen on both a personal level—that may only illustrate my ignorance—and on a social and scientific level. When Duchamp exhibited (or tried to) his urinal, or when Bob Dylan released the single "Like a Rolling Stone," or when Wittgenstein published his *Tractatus*, many had to revise their views of the world. To experience requires the courage to be vulnerable. We always have the truth we deserve in accordance with how flexible we are in our perception of the world. Stubborn people have stubborn truths.

Thus, in order to create freely, there should be no preestablished border. Whereas the designer typically designs with a specific purpose in mind—a spoon to eat with or a chair to sit on—the artist or the philosopher can remain disinterested to such functionality. Art and philosophy challenge our tendency to order and dispute what we take for granted. This is why a good novel or book of philosophy can be a painful encounter; suddenly, the world is no longer what you thought it was. It changes you, changes how you see the world. You can never return.

A metaphysic of becoming confirms that affirming requires that you are free to affirm differences—that is, you are aware that life is difference. Therefore, if you don't allow these difference to flourish, but rather try to make them fit, you are violating life. It is an acknowledgement of that which cannot be placed within a known system of knowledge but is nevertheless there. This requires that you pay attention *openly* to what happens, that you are willing to experiment, and that you are courageous enough to propose alternatives.

* * * *

Deleuze's metaphysics distinguishes him from two other significant thinkers of the 20th century: Martin Heidegger and Ludwig Wittgenstein.

Heidegger claimed, "metaphysics is onto-theology."[27] This suggests that metaphysics is both the study of what is or that which is (i.e., ontology), as well as theology or religion. In other words, the study of being is being conducted with reference to an already given religious order or master plan. Every time we encounter something new, we stop and ask: "Does it fit?" "Can we make it fit?"

Aristotle may have said that a story always has a beginning, middle, and end. The story of life may be organized by some ordering structure, as Heidegger proposes. However, a metaphysic of becoming opens a different story—one with no beginning or end . . . a story that always takes place in the middle. This is another way of not raising birth or especially death to the only (or most) meaningful event in life. We are, after all, always dying because we are also living. Dying and living we can experience consciously, whereas experiencing birth and death is a more debatable question. Life comes from nowhere moving toward everywhere.

In *Tractatus Logico-Philosophicus*, Wittgenstein famously said, "What we cannot speak about we must pass over in silence."[28] What Wittgenstein tried to answer was the following questions: "Is there something which we cannot dispute?" "Is complete certainty possible?" "Can we know the truth?" The conclusion he makes is that there is no truth outside of mathematics or, at least, we cannot grasp the possible truth through language. This conclusion leaves him in a bit of a dilemma: if philosophy is a quest for truth, then philosophical practice is dead. Later, quite originally, Wittgenstein would change his approach and conclusion about philosophy, proposing that meaning depends on the context, not on an ultimate referent.

Science deals with facts; still, there is something that science (at least not yet) or even language can't grasp. Philosophy can be seen as a way of trying to grasp more, for example, through the creation of concepts that can help us see more. "Deleuze sees himself as being strictly *immanent* to metaphysics: creation and transformation are possible within metaphysics, and there are virtualities in past metaphysics that are capable of being reactivated, as it were, and inserted into new contexts, and new problematics. Metaphysics itself, in other words, is dynamic and in constant becoming."[29]

The past, present, and future are negotiable—that is, what there was may change, as it is actualized in the present living moment, making another future possible. To think is an ongoing process of *organizing* where you never reach *the* organization per se, but constantly de-organize and reorganize. What is there is always in the process of becoming, oscillating between what has been and what will be. Even in the sense that we can say, "I would have had a beautiful childhood," becoming moves in both directions.

The metaphysics of becoming also affects how we can think and understand the political concept "utopia."

4

The Utopia of Deleuze's Thought

To AFFIRM IS A UTOPIAN ACTIVITY. THOMAS MOORE coined the word "utopia" in his novel *Utopia*, which refers to
a nearly perfect island positioned in an unknown ocean.
The etymology of the word stresses this ambiguous meaning between *eu*topia = the good place, and *ou*topia = no
place. Thus, utopia is a dream of a good place that does
not exist.

Even though a utopia (i.e., the island in an unknown
ocean) doesn't exist, it can still be powerful as a guiding
idea. It can stimulate and inspire, as well as dominate and
repress. A utopia is a way of giving significance to certain
actions. In literature, as well as in politics, it establishes a
conflict where the utopian island or community attempts
to shed light on the inhuman condition that we currently
live under.

Still, if a utopia is the good place that doesn't exist,

then "utopia is not the best word," write Deleuze and Guattari.[30] Saying this has nothing to do with the fact that Moore coined it in his novel *Utopia*. Fiction is just another resource for insights. There can be just as much knowledge in a novel by Michel Houllebecq as in an academic paper on the sex industry. Instead, what makes a utopian concept problematic is that it refers to a fixed "Other"—for example, the perfect island. It's something transcendent. It is a fantasy, a good place that doesn't exist as anything but an abstract or guiding ideal—that is, as a moral motivator.

So, what should we call it?

Ernst Bloch says "our epoch has brought with it an 'upgrading' of the utopian—only it is not called this anymore. It is called 'science fiction.'"[31] As Bloch predicted, Deleuze and Guattari actually do refer to another science fiction writer, Samuel Butler, and his novel *Erewhon*. The title *Erewhon* is an anagram, it "refers not only to no-where, but also now-here."[32] Instead of seeing utopia as a resolution—an a priori structure that organizes the world (i.e., metaphysic of being)—they see it as an approach or process. To affirm is to embody a certain attitude or relationship with life. Giving direction based on what takes place, here and now. What is also possible? To say it more simply: the aim of a philosophy of mindfulness is to undo or unlearn all the structures that we have wrapped life into.

So, utopia is no longer the good that may or may not exist. It's nowhere and now here. The point is that "now here" is an acceptance that we cannot structure our approach to the world as if we were a tourist looking for *the* island.

"There is no royal road to learning," as Euclid said.

Paying attention, now *and* here, is a way of "travelling back and forward in time all the time and with no need for special machines or for odd physical properties such as wormholes . . . the past, present and future are not separate parts of time."[33] Now and here refers to actualization, making all times contemporary. Even our memories, when they appear, do so in different shapes and colors depending on each new present living moment. Actualization cuts transversally. For example, our past may seem more or less fixed: when, where, how; however if we get rid of all structures and identities that we use to relate to our past, we can actualize the past memories into a present multiplicity. As the saying goes, it is never too late for a good childhood. However, the childhood doesn't improve because we go back with new structural tools that *normalize*; rather, the past comes alive by chance (e.g., a smell, a song, or a face).

"Now here" emphasizes the ongoing zigzagging process of actualization. It stresses how time is more than linear clock time; time is also physics, "an irreversible and irrevocable fluctuating," as Serres says. Time "drifts from order to disorder."[34] The philosophical point is that we can't reduce life to one aspect of reality—for example, the present moment; on the contrary, we are always placed in between past and future, knowledge and ignorance, etc. The less aspect we limit ourselves to engage in, the less we understand. The more complex we can think, the more strength our thoughts have.

* * * *

An affirmative and mindful philosophy is as an engagement with the world—now and here—in order to affect qualitative changes. A potential better future is not just a possibility but also something to be tested and validated through its ongoing actualization. What is better for us to do in this particular moment?

The potential "better" future is unknown until it is being created. Ethics is a risky business. All we can do is to connect "with what is real here and now in the struggle against capitalism, relaunching new struggles whenever the earlier one is betrayed."[35] Traditionally, utopia is a dream with specific conditions that emerge as *daydreaming*, *idealizing*, or *alternative*, all of which may be seen as a way of covering or obscuring what is real. Utopia as "now here" doesn't operate with alternatives; it produces them. Life is virtual—a force or potentiality that is real, but *not yet* actualized. " . . . It is the event that is a meanwhile [*un entre-temps*]: the meanwhile is not part of the eternal, but neither is it a part of time—it belongs to becoming . . ."[36]

You place yourself within the event as you unfold its potential, you engage or involve yourself in life from within life as such, you actualize, in every instant, that *which is* worth actualizing, bring what is living into life. Slowly we take one step at a time into the unknown, investing our life for the sake of life as such. A utopian activity turns out to be an interrogation of life: "How does it work?" "What has just happened?" "What is going to happen?"

What is happening, therefore, is always a mixture of *no longer* and *not yet*.

To actualize is to confirm the becoming in being. Philosophy aims at letting life sprout. This practice is also what makes it ethical and, furthermore, ethical in a generous and highly creative way.

5

The Ethics of Deleuze's Thought

DELEUZE OPERATES WITH AN IMMANENT ETHICS. "IT is only when immanence is no longer immanence to anything other than itself that we can speak of a plane of immanence."[37] Immanence can be described as something existing or "remaining within," "being inherent." Immanence is not only contrasted with transcendence but also with metaphysic questioning as to whether there is something or nothing "beyond." Immanence also contrasts with dualism—for example, whether something only exists in opposition to something else. Dualism is having an effect on how we see right versus wrong, good versus bad, and so on, whereas an immanent ethics attempts to move beyond such dualism. To put it simply: there is no two-world view—only this one, "here now."

Ethics, therefore, is not morality. Morality is defined as a set of constraining rules that both guide and judge our actions and intentions. Here, our actions and intentions are viewed according to transcendent or universal values we have, should, or ought to follow, as if we knew what was good or bad beforehand. Morality belongs to the sphere of the quiz show, where you already know the answers to your questions. Ethics, on the other hand, is a set of assisting rules that help you evaluate what you are doing, thinking, and feeling according to the immanent existence it implies.

Morality and ethics can be seen as two different ways of addressing life. One question is, "How should you act (Morality)?" Another question is, "How might you live (Ethics)?" Another way of formulating these questions could be, "What ought we to do? (Morality)" and "What might we also do (Ethics)?"

Ethical questions do not encourage you to steal or loot or claim that slavery or racism is not morally wrong. Of course not. More strongly, it views such postulates as ignorant and without any empirical verification. Slavery and racism only imprison life because they don't view all lives as being equal. Norms, however, are potentially changeable; if viewed as otherwise, they hinder our human curiosity to improve from within life. The current values and norms are respected but not spared or preserved. Nietzsche called this practice to "philosophize with the hammer," which is a practice that begins by acknowledging that the notion of value implies a critical reversal.

"The problem of critique is that of the value of values, of the evaluation from which their values arises, thus the problem of their *creation*. Evaluation is defined as the differential element of corresponding values, an element that is both critical and creative. Evaluations, in essence, are not values but ways of being, modes of existence of those who judge and evaluate, serving as principles for the values on the basis of which they judge. This is why we always have the beliefs, feelings and thoughts that we deserve given our way of being or our style of life. There are things that can only be said, felt or conceived, values which can only be adhered to, on condition of 'base' evaluation, 'base' living and thinking."[38]

* * * *

A typical ethical challenge is how to overcome yourself—that is, overcome your will to the truth—for example, the unquestionable faith in certain ideologies or norms. Favoring a particular ideology affects how you perceive the world. To evaluate, on the other hand, is to create. This means that you create a site or temporary plane where things can emerge as something different depending on the forces or strengths that take possession of it. It is a site where what becomes can express itself. In other words, you don't evaluate based on taxonomies or systems of classification, because regardless of how convenient such models are, they are essentially reductionist. They try to label what is moving instead of following the flow of life.

Ethics, then, is a matter of power or strength, a will to power that should not be interpreted as what the will wants but the one that wants in the will . . . a will to create or invent. To seek power, for instance, power over, is the lowest degree of the will to power. To make a person do what that person would not otherwise do is an example of power over. Basically, the will to power tries to overcome the habit of what might be called "the will to truth." An example could be when a theory looks for confirmation of its own claims. "What a will wants is to affirm its differen-ce"[39]—that is, the differences that emerge when different forces encounter one another. "In order to be actualized, the virtual cannot proceed by elimination or limitation, but must *create* its own lines of actualization in positive acts."[40]

The criterion of what to affirm is related to strengths or the power to act. Thus, selecting a choice is not im-plicitly closing down other potential choices. Instead, making a decision is to liberate yourself because you are enhancing your capability to act. Each decision you make in life makes your life freer. Or to put it simply: the decisions that you make today make it easier to make decisions tomorrow. To philosophize is about becoming free of everything . . . becoming free of what you know. Do today what you, based on your current knowledge, would also do tomorrow. It is both a critical and yet positive approach to life because it doesn't settle.

* * * *

The normative formulation of an immanent ethic is: "Do you desire this once more and innumerable times more?"[41] Or "*whatever you will, will it in such a way that you also will its eternal return.*"[42]

The term "whatever you will" may sound careless or even egoistic. Therefore, to avoid any misunderstandings, if anyone wishes to discriminate against women because "one will" or reduce all men to male chauvinists, then this person cannot do so without reducing him or herself to an ignorant person. Who would like to continue being ignorant? The point is that an immanent ethics doesn't abandon the existing practical reason; however, it doesn't see the practical knowledge as finished. You cannot will what you cannot do (basically, there is something diminishing in acting stupid, e.g., claiming there is a gender theory when all there is are gender studies and so forth, or claiming that the climate problem is not caused by humans). Instead, this ethical and immanent approach to life aims at improving your capacity to act, hereby learning the best ways of doing things, noticing how this "best way" changes due to new experiments. Therefore, knowledge is normative, but if you can do better, then this improvement also changes the norm. Similarly, if you can, then it makes sense to will it unless norms or political democratic agendas are hindering your power to act.

Furthermore, this approach stresses how a force is "what can"—for instance, a force can do something or affect a person, whereas the will to power is "what will." In other words, do what you will, but only insofar as you *can* exercise this will at this specific moment. Most children learn this practice quite fast. Often children believe that because they will or want something, then it is in their right to receive it. Sometimes, even parents quite ridiculously tell their children that they can do whatever they will. However, gradually, the children learn—we all learn—that they cannot do everything they will. To live well is also to acknowledge your failure. This is the key to living a good life.

Recapitulating, you first need to be affected by the

outside; here mindfulness can help make us more aware. Then, we have to see whether we can actually match what is happening; here lies the notion "will what you can" (or accept what you can't). This willingness, however, is creative and rebellious; it refuses to just give up and follow the herd, and so while you acknowledge your failures, you also move on. Moving on is doing what you will also repeat tomorrow, and the day after, and so forth.

* * * *

"Either ethics makes no sense at all, or this is what it means and has nothing else to say: not to be unworthy of what happens to us. To grasp whatever happens as unjust and unwarranted (it is always someone else's fault) is, on the contrary, what renders our sores repugnant—veritable *ressentiment*, resentment of the event. There is no other ill will. What is really immoral is the use of moral notions like just or unjust, merit or fault."[43]

It is easy, perhaps even comfortable, to judge. That is, to speak before really tasting the food. It can give you an idea of belonging to a higher, more lucrative position. However, philosophy as a way of living emphasizes that "to taste" is refining our bodily sensations. "We are too quick to forget that *homo sapiens* refers to those who act to sapidity, appreciate and seek it out, those for whom the sense of taste matters— savouring animals—before referring to judgment . . . *wisdom comes after taste.*"[44]

To rely on your sensory experience and not just confirm what you're taught to expect is a way of engaging with the world. Affirming, therefore, is to accept setbacks such as "war, wounds, and death"; to accept what awaits us: "to become the offspring of one's own events, and thereby to be reborn, to have one more birth, and to break with one's carnal birth—to become the offspring of one's events and not of one's actions, for the action is itself produced by the offspring of the event."[45] As I mentioned previously, acknowledging our failures is part of maturing, and detaching knowledge from our deceptions on a personal as well as social level. Why does someone believe that the climate changes are not our responsibility? Is it because we can't see how the present living moment is connected with the past and future generations?

Serres mentions how animals "wolf down their food," whereas "man tastes it."[46] Does the human really taste the food that he or she eats? This line of thought can easily be extended, questioning how much of life we actually taste—that is, experience, experiment with, and actualize. It is not just shallowness that has reduced our ability to taste; it is related to how the culture of taste tends to be expressed in a specialized language that can discriminate. Imagine a wine taster who doesn't speak French! This is again related to our obsessive achievement society where we often don't have the time to practice—that is, taste and experience life. Instead, we run to the nearest guide, hoping to get the answer to "What is the right thing to do?"

The event is happening, but it is also as something that is already anticipated. Epictus says, "Do not seek to have everything that happens happen as you wish, but wish for everything to happen as it actually does happen, and your life will be serene."[47]

Imagine that the wine you bought to impress your friends is rather awful. It does not live up to what "the judge" claimed in the shop. Here, everything is not happening as you hoped for; still, we are encouraged to wish for everything to happen as it actually did. Why? First of all, to accept that there are things that we cannot change; second, to really taste this rather distasteful moment as a way of enhancing reality. Instead of just pitying your own vanity wounds, blaming the connoisseur in the winery, this particular moment is an invitation to know life as such . . . to move beyond yourself.

Moving beyond yourself is to become *with,* becoming other. It is acknowledging the freedom related to the fact that "you do not know beforehand what good or bad you are capable of; you do not know beforehand what a body or mind can do, in a given encounter, a given arrangement, a given combination."[48]

What is there to do? Experience, ask questions, experiment, see what is worth actualizing for the sake of the next generations.

BELIEVE IN THIS WORLD

6

TOGETHER WITH GUATTARI, DELEUZE BEGAN the book *A Thousand Plateaus* in the following manner: "The two of us wrote *Anti-Oedipus* together. Since each of us was already several, there was already a crowd . . ."

They kept their names out of habit, not because one is not the other, but rather, because each one is many. They want to reach the point "where one no longer says I, but the point where it is no longer of any importance whether one says I. We are no longer ourselves."[49] This is becoming imperceptible . . . the space where you can be inventive and creative—that is, enlarge your capacity to experience. "A depersonalization of the self, in a gesture of everyday transcendence of the ego, is a connecting force, a binding force that links the self to larger internal and external relations."[50]

Due to the encounters that we have, for instance, through mental exercises such as meditation, we are able to connect or relate to something that is not us. To be even more precise: the fixed distinction between you and me, the world and me, becomes blurry—that is, impercepti-ble. It does not make sense to claim, "This is who I am" because I am changing. It is not about who we are or what we would like to be; rather, it is about what we are capable of becoming. Becoming is a never-ending process. There is no end goal or ideal "self"; it always depends on the unfolding of the here and now.

Thus, if we are no longer ourselves, we are free to become whomever. Therefore, when the two Frenchmen literally claim to be several—a multiplicity—they pro-pose that names are just a convenient habitual reference and not something that gives access to an extraordinary destiny (as some parents believe when they name their children). No one is a given—he or she is understood as an unchangeable and stable entity, an essence; rather, each one of us is a process . . . a *changing process*. We are mutants. A mutant is not only, as Hollywood has made us believe, a brutal beast; on the contrary, a mutant is *extra-ordinary*, heteromorphic, and unconventional.

"Philosophy does not consist in knowing and is not inspired by truth. Rather, it is categories like Interesting, Remarkable, or Important that determine success or failu-re. Now, this cannot be known before being constructed."[51] As the philosopher—or the rest of us—intervenes metaphysically in the world, he or she may fabricate or invent concepts that sometimes succeed and sometimes fail. It depends on the sustainability of the process of actualization, which illustrates that exploring is an open and singular process.

Since each of us is already several, what matters is to experience a contact or an intimate relation with life where it is no longer important who is saying what, only what and how things are being said.

What difference does it make who is speaking?

* * * *

"We no longer live in a disciplinary society controlled by prohibitions or commands, but rather in an achievement-orientated society that is allegedly free," said philosopher Byung-Chul Han.[52] He continued, "Yes, we presume ourselves to be free, but in reality we voluntarily and passionately exploit ourselves until we collapse."

Han has, in several essays, expressed how today's neoliberalism has made politics psychological or mental. This critique also affects mindfulness in that it claims (like Buddhism) that every suffering in life is mental. Imagine that you have lost your job or can't find a job, and as a consequence you have to live with your parents at the age of 40 (not unrealistic in Spain), you can't hang out with your friends because you don't have the few Euros needed to buy a coffee, and you are viewed with pity as if a person without an income or a job is a person without life. This suffering is not solely mental but is also mostly social. It is initiated by a capitalistic ideology that measures human lives in terms of human capital; it's a world governed by money, property, and goods. Thus, to philosophize is also to go against the growing tendency to make all social or political problems mental.

The logic of neoliberalism has invaded our minds. It's our ability to be present in our life, to think, and to love that is threatened by this invasion. We shrink mentally because we are no longer capable of thinking movement. Instead, we are being managed or you manage yourself as if life were lived running around in a ring. We run and run, unable to stop due to centrifugal force that just makes us addicted to being on the run, being online, being absentminded, until one day our body collapses.

How can we open us towards what is happening, allowing ourselves to be moved by life and being uncritically moved around by ideologies?

Spirituality refers to the breeze of life that may move minds. Thus, when we do not allow ourselves to be affected by external life forces, we shrink. If we only move to please the dominating consensus or "fit in" with "good company," then we are not free. Often our moves are forced or controlled by society's norms and ideals, or our own ideals and norms (which again are colored by society's), to perform or achieve something specific.

Nowadays, we have become narcissists in two ways that may overlap. On the one side, many are very preoccupied with themselves—for example, as seen in self-help literature where people are encouraged to love themselves before anyone else. On the other side, more and more people are desperately seeking confirmation and recognition from others—for example, through various forms of exposure to obtain attention. The desire to be recognized and to gain status in the eyes of others is, to some extent, just self-love; both are unhealthy. Instead of this ridiculous hunt to be somebody, there is something liberating in abandoning the idea of a true self in favor of becoming. Such a process is impersonal and, therefore, less stressful. Stress and burnout should not be seen as individual or personal breakdowns; on the contrary, they are related to the overall breakdown of society and its obsessive growth mantra. For instance, in a lot of self-help literature and coaching, the mantra is "to become the best you" or "realize your true potential"; both are competitive in a way that is strange for a philosophy of life. Competition is objectifying. Although it makes sense to have clear objectives in football, life can't be objectified mainly because you can't participate fully if you objectify your own life. This is also the problem when people interpret what they have done in an attractive self-centered narrative.

While continuing this competition to be the best performer, we lack a critical yet creative approach to overcome this confinement—for example, a critical view of how many people look at themselves as objects. We have to learn to think more self-critically . . . free ourselves from "the terror of positivity," as Han has described it.[53] He describes our current society as one "dominated by a surplus of positivity, even in one's own affective household. It seems negative feelings are an impediment to accelerating the process. The utmost in acceleration can be expected where the same answers to the same. Negativity slows down and prevents a chain reaction of sameness... Depression is a disease of the narcissistic self that has been set adrift from relationships, that has lost all sense of what is different. The virtual space is a hell of sameness."

To criticize begins with acknowledging how we might be terrorized by smiley's and thumbs-up, and yet, we may also participate in this terror. Han notes that we are forced or coerced into participating in ongoing positive communication, declaring "I like" over and over again and again. There seems to be a general conviction that we *ought* to share our lives on the Internet or the conviction that we *should* like the photos of our friends. Such conviction can easily turn into a moralizing domination, where you may be forced to explain why you don't want to share. Furthermore, an uncritical positivity is nothing but resentment. Social media directly and indirectly forces people to communicate more. Updates and news drop down quickly; you need to keep adding new communications in order to remain visible. A non-visible person is a nonexistent person. Therefore, we communicate without having anything to say other than: "Look, I am still alive", "Look, I am here." It's a childish need for attention and recognition. It is exhausting. We all need recognition and confirmation, but as we mature, we get it more from consciously experiencing being connected with life. The moral seems to be the following: The more you scream for attention and recognition, the less alive you are.

* * * *

Philosophy is an intervening time. A time of "non-doing" and "a peace time," as Han described it. The concept of "non-doing" also resembles elements of mindfulness in that it stresses that we don't need to be doing things constantly. Life is not a competition. Why rush for the final *dead*line? We do not need to do something specific, just as we do not have to do what is expected of us whether forced by society or ourselves. Non-doing allows things to unfold at their own pace.

Similarly, Hartmut Rosa, in *Social Acceleration—A New Theory of Modernity*, shows how acceleration influences our lives. Systematically, he shows the causes and consequences of an acceleration that doesn't stop for anything. He identifies three categories of change: technological acceleration (e.g., transportation and communication), social change (e.g., knowledge), and pace of life. Rosa borrows his underlying thesis from his German colleague Luhmann: "the division of time and value judgment can no longer be separated."[54] The moral is, therefore, that how we spend our time shows what we value. Time becomes the most valuable once we see life as something that ends. The prophecy of Benjamin Franklin's "time is money" has, unfortunately, come true. Because even though we value being with our children, many also feel obliged to be productive within a capitalistic framework (or when they are with their children, the intensity is low because their mind is elsewhere, for example, "at work"). A simple way to reflect on the way you use your time is to see whether your thoughts, feelings, and actions cohere. Do your thinking and living hang together?

We have forgotten the benefits of non-doing; we have become too impatient to wait. Sometimes, a new gaze is born out of waiting, what before was invisible to us suddenly steps out of the painting. Or while we wait, just sitting there on the bench without checking news on our phones, we surpass our ignorance while experiencing if nothing else then the fact that time endures. Waiting, therefore, is not refusing to act, but to dwell on the moment, stretching it in order to respond more wisely. Unfortunately, waiting, patience, and unlimited attention are articles in short supply today.

Rosa suggests that "the qualities of 'our times,' its horizons and structures, its tempo and its rhythm, are not (or only to a very limited degree) at our disposal. Temporal structures have a collective nature and social character."[55] It means that in order to change how it may also be possible to live, it is not enough to "just" change your own way of living because you are being formed by the social structures as well. On the contrary, by changing the social structures, you are able to alter the conditions that may affect you. Instead of speeding up, when you're met with a stressing deadline, you could take a moment to do nothing. In other words, we have to be aware not to confuse sense with signification. There is "no structure without the empty square, which makes everything function."[56] To sense, therefore, is not to perceive, but rather to be aware of how we tend to perceive the world.

Are we spending our lives in concordance with what we value? Are there things we silently pass on to the next generation because we don't dare revolt? Are we postponing living until life has lived itself by using all its strengths and energies? Could I use my time differently?

Everything is encapsulated in time. We cannot step outside of time. Just as nature doesn't guarantee what is good or bad, the Internet that facilitates much of human interaction today is also not morally good or bad per se. Proposing such a value judgment makes as much sense as suggesting that electricity is morally good or bad. Instead it's how we use the Internet. Perhaps due to the anonymity that the Internet provides, it generates both generous sharing of knowledge and the most unpleasant sides of human behavior. The challenge is how to merge abstractions or norms with a concrete situational practice. Time alters everything; it affects us.

Norms are social artifacts, not something sacred and unchangeable. Norms are components of practical knowledge. Acting conscientious is an ongoing effort. The practical knowledge of a community changes due to its practical reasoning. "Practical reasoning at its best is improvisational and creative."[57] Expectations and perceptions are tested. Whether we produce new knowledge depends on our involvement that stems from our will to interpret life unarmed (e.g., without following habits or fixed sets of guidelines), as well as our ability to create new values.

* * * *

Time is change. A society is always transforming: reproduction without sex, feminism without women, alcohol-free beer, coffee without caffeine, wisdom without wrinkles. Rosa's thesis is that acceleration affects us personally and socially. This is again related to business, where time is money measured through efficiency. There is an underlying norm related to acceleration: Because we can, we must (Han makes a similar point in *Mudigkeitsgesselchaft*). Seen from a distance, we notice a movement away from a disciplinary society where everyone was institutionalized and where the institutions told us: You shall. Today, the disciplinary society has become one of control. Here, the mantra is "You can, therefore, you should." This mantra affects everything from work to sex: "Because I can work now, I should", "Because I can have sex with many, I should." This mantra is the reason why we exploit ourselves until we collapse. It resembles those microeconomic studies of people's behavior comparing when they are ordering just a pizza to when they are eating at establishments where you can eat what you can for 10 Euro. The notion "what you can" makes many people eat more than they actually can eat, just as some work more, although it actually drains them. This is not just because of the time used, but is also due to the energy used, the level of intensity, and mental activity we pressure ourselves to cope with.

When everything speeds up, it can be difficult to stay calm offline. This is due to the "shrinking of the present" that we can see different forms of counter movements, such as slow living and mindfulness, that try to convince us that if we pay attention to each moment, then the chance of forgetting something important is less likely—for example, forgetting to live. There is also a high level of gratitude related to these moments. Rosa proposes the concept of resonance, which is actually a way of flowing with time—that is, where time is seen as an intense rhythm and where you experience being in harmony with life. Resonance is not an emotional state but is characterized by being touched or marked by something in an active or involved way that affects or changes you. It could be by reading a book or lying in your bed with your child while you consciously experience how your child and your own breathing tally with one another. Rosa ends with a quote from an author saying that, "the acceleration society gets people 'to will what they do not will,' that is, to pursue . . . courses of action that they do not prefer from a temporal stable perspective." This is an example of control.

Still, to will something else requires a will to power—that is, a will to be affected. An affirmative philosophy requires our full attention toward what life is becoming. Blanchot writes, "In attention, the center of attention disappears, the central point around which perspective, sight, and the order of that which is to be seen inwardly and outwardly are distributed."58 In other words, moral markers, dominating tastes, or any other fixed signposts do not guide our attention. He continues, "Mystery: its essence is always on this side of attention. And the essence of attention is the ability to preserve, in and through itself, that which is always on this side of attention and the source of all waiting: mystery. Attention, the welcoming of that which escapes attention, an opening onto the unexpected, waiting that is the unexpected in all waiting."

It's a mystery that people don't want more out of life than recognition for their position in the capitalistic system, rather than their posture toward life.

Thus, it is not more moralism that is needed; rather, it is more creativity. Part of being creative is slowing down, being capable of wasting time—that is, doing unfunctional things. This may sound like another romantic idea similar to the view of the artist that I presented at the beginning of this book. For example, Rousseau in his *Emilie* speaks about how children learn when they waste time—that is, when they are not measured and evaluated constantly according to some performance ideal. I agree with Rousseau. However, unlike Rousseau, I don't wish to return to a more primitive or "natural" state of life; rather, to reinvent the world. This is where we can learn from art. Wasting time, therefore, depends on how we define waste. The point I wish to make is that it requires a more flexible relationship with life to allow yourself to be formed or touched by what is happening as it happens, without judging it according to some predefined ideal. Throw away the compass with a fixed needle (e.g., the compass given by religion or any other moral institution), get lost for a while, and then reinvent or reorganize your relationship with life.

Accordingly, Han's philosophy, like most forms of mindfulness meditation, tries to advocate for non-doing. Most of his critique is realized as practice. Han points out liberating lines of flight that can change our relation with the world—for example, that it is okay not to do anything. Instead of being exhausted, he suggests that it is okay to be tired. That is, within the draining element that fuels today's achievement society also lies the possibility to let go . . . to become whatever. It is okay to be too tired to be exhausted.

We live in a narcissistic culture. Like Narcissus, more and more people fall into the water and drown. However, narcissism is a double sword: we want to look good in the eyes of others. The moral seems to be I love myself because I am so good, just, sexy, smart, and fair in the eyes of others.

Unfortunately, such a moral only leads to decay as all forms of ego trips, whereas love in a spiritual context always honors interconnectedness.

7

A FEW YEARS BACK, KABAT-ZINN WROTE TOGETHER WITH Professor in Clinical Psychology, Mark Williams, that "the rush to define mindfulness within Western psychology may wind up denaturing it in fundamental ways" [59] mainly because of the underlying norms or ideas of "normality" that psychologists use for diagnosis. The risk is that mindfulness is squeezed into a setting that is not open, whereto it becomes a tool for something specific, whereas it is actually a practice on non-doing, leading to nowhere specific. The two authors continue asking whether there is "the potential for something priceless to be lost."

It's the radical openness that risks being lost, as well as an affirmative practice that embraces life. The affirmation takes places in between "'no longer' and the 'not yet' i.e. between a proliferation of possibilities and a degree zero of self-presence." [60] The risk of relating philosophy with mindfulness is, however, the self-presence of the meditator. For example, in mindfulness, subjectivity often coincides with a conscious autonomous agency, whereas Deleuze's philosophy "map[s] the non-human becomings of life."[61] Becomings, therefore, consider all organisms—plants and animals—as an equal part of life. Therefore, it is a direct connection with life.

Then, if we turn mindfulness into a norm, it hinders its own requirements of openness, curiosity, and respect for life. It may hinder the free flow of life. The benefits of practicing mindfulness, for example, depend on our attitude or approach, not on what system of thoughts we represent. Thus, mindfulness can only help us in becoming a seer, if it lets go of its own desire to see itself as a universal remedy. Can we accept that problems are not either mental or political but often much more difficult to distinguish? Camus once said, "It is a kind of spiritual snobbery that makes people think they can be happy without money." This is not suggesting that money can buy you love or happiness, but that contemporary life is permeated with money that often functions as a kind of access or password to education, health care, even to "good" company, and, of course, all the basic needs, such as food and shelter. Without a social commitment, and outward as well as inward look, mindfulness can turn into a remedy for self-development for the privileged middle class in the Western world. For some, there may even be status or prestige in claiming "I am spiritual," whereas what matters is the person's mind-set and attitude to life.

An affirmative philosophy emphasizes this responsibility because a philosopher exposes himself or herself to get in contact with life and not some predefined idea or knowledge about life or how life should be lived. This is risky. Yet, philosophy is about trusting this life that we live in this world. "Belief is no longer addressed to a different or transformed world. Man is in the world as if in a pure optical and sound situation. The reaction to which man has been disposed can be replaced only by belief. Only belief in the world can reconnect man to what he sees and hears."[62]

Establishing such belief is an ethical process.

* * * *

To live ethically is not to be unworthy of what happens. Ethics is a form of life worthy of accepting what life has to offer. Not worthy in the sense that you should live up to certain ideals or norms, but rather that you are capable of embracing what actually takes place. Carry your experiences with you. Regardless of what happens, you should still believe in this world. There is no other world. Mindfulness shares this acceptance, which it tries to cultivate or nurture through the training of your concentration, attention, and observation. It matters whether you pay attention or not. Therefore, seeing mindfulness as both an inward and outward practice may help us comprehend what happens to us but also release or set free the becomings of what is happening. By doing so, we become the results of relating or connecting with these becomings, not our actions. Our actions are responses to what is happening. For this simple reason, you also care for what takes place while it is taking place.

Awareness and affirmation go hand in hand. Before you actualize what is in the process of coming into being, you register it. "We need an ethic or a faith, which makes fools laugh; it is not a need to believe in something else, but a need to believe in this world, of which fools are a part… The modern fact is that we no longer believe in this world. We do not even believe in the events which happen to us, love, death, as if they only half concerned us."[63]

Thus, the right thing to do is to believe in a world that is constantly becoming something else. This requires awareness. To establish or reestablish a belief "not in a different world, but the link between man and the world, in love or life, to believe in this as in the impossible, the unthinkable, which none the less cannot but be thought: 'something possible, otherwise I will suffocate.'"[64] In order not to suffocate, you must breathe. It may not establish a belief in this world, but it is vital. It keeps you in this world. This is it. After a while, most people accept that this is it; if not, your life crumbles away while you are planning something magnificent or feeling sorrow for all your losses.

Future regrets can only be avoided in the actualization of present moments.

Most exercises in mindfulness begin with something like "Sit down and follow your breath." The breath is like an anchor. Even though your mind is drifting like a canoe on a turbulent river, you can bring your attention back to your breath. It is a way of noticing that you are here, even if you can't handle what happens and would rather escape from this moment, it actually still happens. An affirmative philosophy is one that can help each of us to become worthy of what happens to us as well as the others. It can turn transformation into something natural. Still, if the transformation or actualization or becoming is to be sustainable and responsible, it is important that the process is impersonal—that is, becomes imperceptible.

* * * *

What does it mean to believe in this world? It's an

effort more than an unshakable faith. An example is how the work of the writer Terry Tempest Williams deals with reestablishing and recreating the intimacy between all living beings, as well as with the earth. She practices a sensuous and generous ethic. "I trust what I see. The surface of things is what we see," she writes and continues, "I trust what I touch. The surface of things is what we touch."[65]

To believe is not to look for something deeper; it's not a play between signifier and signification. Rather, it is to use our senses: "what my eyes can see, what my fingers can touch, what my hand can know by moving slowly across the flesh, or fur, or feathers, or stone." It is a mixture of knowing *that* and knowing *how*. For example, you can't invent an experience without having experienced it. See what emerges.

When Williams looks out on the prairie, she notices, "Prairie dogs have a significant effect of biological diversity in prairie ecosystems. More than 200 species of wildlife have been associated with prairie dog towns, with over 140 species benefiting directly . . ." Prairie dogs create diversity. Destroy them, and you destroy a varied world. She emphasizes that the "prairie dog lives because of community." Similarly, we human beings cannot live without a community—that is, someone who takes care of us, helps us, knows other things that we do, etc. It is also here that neoliberals often forget that no one becomes rich alone because they use the infrastructure that society made for them, use the competences that society has gradually verified, and so forth.

Another interesting feature of prairie dogs is that their skulls have enormous eye sockets. "What they see and how fast they see" is part of their survival. Basically, they are on the lookout for enemies, as well as food and shelter. They are on the lookout for who needs extra care and attention. The moral is: If we—the people in general—do not see, we do not survive. However, seeing means understanding how, for example, the diversity of ideas and forms of life are related to care, not competition. Similarly, it stresses how we have to take care of the prairie dogs because we are in it together. They are a part of us.

Williams asks, "What is our definition of development?" Today, the answer seems to be almost exclusively related to economic growth. She asks, "What is sustainable development?", "What kind of world do we want to create?", and "What kind of world are we creating?"

These questions intervene directly with what is not yet over and what has not yet come into being. What is dying and what is being born refer to ideas or current modes of existence. It could be how different forms of communications (e.g., pre-Internet and post-Internet) may change our behavior and address new needs (e.g., pursuit of silence or off-line space). It forces us to reflect upon our contribution, as well as accountability for the status quo. The kind of life we live affects the world we live in, and vice versa. There is nothing sustainable in economic growth. Money doesn't have any other value than what we ascribe to it. To be of value, money needs a material reference. Unfortunately, we don't often look at the value of working, helping, and servicing other people unless we can attach such actions and gestures to a monetary value. Managerial practices, such as human resource management and performance management, are ways of reducing the human being to a resource, as if the experiences of each human being (i.e., its various forms of life) could be measured as human capital. It is no big surprise that half of the workforce in the Western world is stressed. We have forgotten that we, like the prairie dogs, live because of the communities . . . or to put it more clearly, we get stressed, depressed, and suffer from burnout because of the communities that we are forced to live in. The only way to deal with a controlling and repressive world is to become so free that your form of life can't be capitalized.

If our actions, thoughts, and feelings occur in response to certain circumstances, it is necessary to see what our behavior is within these circumstances. Life works through affects; for example, we cannot just build shopping malls everywhere, because then the prairie dog will become extinct, and if the prairie dogs are extinct, then between 150 and 200 species will be, too. "If you take away all the prairie dogs, there will be no one to cry for the rain."

Instead of organizing our lives based on needs or in terms of means and ends, such as people as means to fulfill certain ends, then a free life is lived according to a production, a productivity, a potency, in terms of causes and effects.

The difference between marketing needs for the sake of profit versus a life lived more in alignment with basic causes and effects is one of competition. When needs only produce profit, then another person anywhere else can carry them out. This is why an achievement society is competitive. An ongoing competition in basically all aspects of life is not only draining but also objectifying "my" relationship with myself—that is to say, my manners of living. So what is beneficial for me and society as such depends on my gestures, my acts, and how I live. Therefore, it would be not only impossible, but also an act of resignation if I were to delegate or outsource my life to another. This is why the mind-set of capitalism is so devastating for our well-being, because it claims that "I" can become whoever "I" want (i.e., typically wanting to become a success according to the performance ideals operating within an obsessed achievement society), whereas what I aim at is to liberate "myself" from this bondage and become *with* life.

Go where life takes you.

Similarly, what Williams is pleading for is an ethic that deals with the human being's relationship with life—that is, the earth and other sentient beings. Nature, however, should not be seen as something original or sacred. Nature is also culture. We may say that everything is culture since our knowledge, belief, laws, and habits of living constantly change. Still, there is a difference in changing every relationship through the gaze of capitalism or through the rhythm of life. The problem is that we often blindly follow the dominating norms of a capitalistic achievement society, where concepts such as freedom, security, value, and growth are reduced to mean "economic freedom," "economic security," "economic wealth," and "economic growth." This is unhealthy. Unfortunately, we have lost our intimacy with life because in between the world as such and me (e.g., other people, the people to come, etc.), our relationship with life has turned into a transaction.

How do we bring back the intimacy?

8

NON-DUALITY MEANS "NOT TWO" OR "NON-SEPARATION." The concept stresses that all things are interconnected, not separate, while at the same time all things retain their singularity. There is not one without another, but the one is not the other. Each one of us is already several. Non-duality refers to an ongoing state of becoming. That is, just becoming as in potentially being many, a multiplicity. The process of becoming does not end; for example, you can't become woman per se, because each woman already is a multiplicity. Such an example also stresses why becoming can liberate us from rigid gender identities and stereotypes. Every human being is a dynamic process, not a fixed identity. As Virginia Woolf writes in *Mrs. Dalloway*—referring to Mrs. Dalloway becoming imperceptible—she would not say of herself, "I am this, I am that, he is this, he is that."[66]

Life is unstable. The foundation is a metaphysic of

becomings that forces us not just to grasp this movement, but also to move with it. This is a classical anthropological experience. You may assume that you speak from the same position as always as if you were your position (or you act as the position predescribes). Yet, just as the anthropologist is formed by his or her audience, the surroundings, and so on, I, too, am being affected. Still, what I propose is that we become more conscious of our own habitual perception because they can sometimes work like armor. The point is not to know exactly what you are (since we are already many); rather, to be open to becoming someone else . . . someone you were not before and someone you don't know who is. That is not only to experience life but also to experiment with it (what is possible?) and make decisions today that you would also repeat tomorrow based on your current knowledge and life situation.

To live free is like writing and love. It is worth doing insofar as we don't know where it will end. You don't get married by studying the statistics of divorces but by loving your partner. You don't write to achieve what the readers want but to explore the limits between what is sayable and non-sayable . . . to investigate and explore life.

Life is a rhizome, which is characterized by having "no beginning or end; it is always in the middle, between things, interceding, *intermezzo*."⁶⁷ It is growing in between other forms of life for which reason becomings is something social or collective (cf. apersonal or impersonal). A rhizome is a creeping and unhierarchical mass of roots that functions like a machine; it is a condition for communication . . . for contact. The human being lives through contact. Consciousness, for example, is not something that happens inside our brain. Instead, it is something that happens to the mind and body. Consciousness is not about; it is becoming. What happens is not being subjected in the body or in the flesh. Instead, sensation functions by itself. "It is the painter that becomes blue."[68] This means that the painter both develops his or her body, for example, by becoming receptive, as well as the painter is being developed into what he or she becomes. The blue period of Picasso is about the painter becoming blue and not the painting about being blue.

The mind, as I understand it, is roughly the same as consciousness and is not something we can look into by dissecting our brain. Also, sensation is not the body but the compound of nonhuman forces such as "blue." So, instead of dissecting our brain or seeing our body as a canvas, it is more helpful to unfold the context that affects the mind and the body—the encounters. Then, we can better understand how we are affected, where, and when. Philosophy explores what we are doing while we are doing it. It's a process, not a theory about what is and how well this or that fits. This is not the same as anything goes, rather, we should evaluate continuously. Evaluations are not checking whether certain values are maintained, but are the conduct of those who evaluate. This is why we have the beliefs, feelings, and thoughts that we deserve given our style of life. Living and thinking go hand in hand. Our thoughts and feelings affect how we experience life. For this reason, it is useful to familiarize yourself with how thoughts and feelings emerge—how these constitute you without identifying with them. This is another aspect where mindfulness can help.

Accordingly, if mindfulness and philosophy convince us, it is not because both have a long tradition of wise men and women; rather, it is because of their concrete effects. Can it help us to live a life of greater connection with all forms of life? Can it help us see what needs to be done—that is, what we have to affirm and what we have to close? Can it help us establish a sustainable future, not just for my children (i.e., vanity) but also for the species as a whole?

* * * *

Each one of us is already participating in life. Thus, mindfulness attends to the reality—for example, my mind—but also the context in which I am placed. That is my mind is placed somewhere geographically, just as it is affected by gender, ethnicity, and age. There are things that I can't change, for example, that I was born in Denmark, but I can always change my relationship with life by actualizing other dimensions.

For example, I don't ask: What does it mean to "come from" Denmark? Rather, I ask: What kind of problem does the notion "come from" produce? To "come from" might imply an original, true, or authentic idea of what it means to be a Dane. Such a norm, of course, can easily break the flow of life. Is a misfit Dane still a Dane?

As you gradually become more mindful due to your engagement or interactions with the world, your level of mindfulness changes (unless you are guided by a norm), which also affects your history because you may understand the past differently. This process resembles the artists who reduce the material to expand the expression. Sometimes, it can be easier to understand the later work of some philosophers because each work is a condensation of the difference that made their thoughts possible. Yet, without seeing this in a context of gradual development, it can perhaps be seen as naïve or even banal at times. Similarly, an artistic example could be the "Dogme 95 Manifesto," created by film director Lars von Trier and Thomas Vinterberg, which prevented the use of special effects, standing cameras, voice-over, artificial light or sound, etc. This approach often awakened something else, which was there already, for example, another way of using and incorporating the setting.

Mindfulness is also something quite simple that you do through training, practice, and nurturing where you gradually become more conscious of what is happening and how well you play along with it. Another way of understanding the mind and body is to see their connection as a machine. Thus, a machine is not something mechanical or predictable that reproduces. On the contrary, a machine creates a new reality, actualizing new ways of being. Everything is a machine merging and merging until it breaks and another merger is possible. Life is machinic—that is, in the midst of becoming something else due to its connections or *relationality*.

What does a machine do? "It breathes, it heats, it eats. It shits and fucks. What a mistake to have ever said *the* id. Everywhere *it* is machines—real ones, not figurative ones: machines driving other machines, machines being driven by other machines, with all the necessary couplings and connections . . . The breast is a machine that produces milk, and the mouth a machine coupled to it."[69]

A machine is a process of production. Each one of us melts with the other to the degree that we can no longer distinguish the one from the other but can only speak of becoming. Philosophy is a machine that couples with other machines, such as thoughts, ideas, books, films, movements, in order to express how thinking is possible. The encounter is where everything begins and dies.

Investigation of such encounters or meetings between people and ideas is linked with creation. Philosophy produces an image of the relation—this vibrating membrane in between inside and outside. Sense is the potentiality for relations. It is impersonal. It is the *and*, where we connect and consciously experience how things work, instead of desperately looking for an already given meaning. There is something liberating in accepting that everything is changing.

Philosophy, therefore, frees knowledge from superstitious beliefs or ideas—for example, the idea that the human being consists of a stable and unchangeable self, as if we all had a little original essence placed deep inside somewhere . . . a mini Finn inside just like how a minibar in a hotel room is only a vague image of the bar in the foyer. Machines illustrate that each relation is nurtured by care and compassion; for example, the baby feeds at the breast because it brings the mother and the baby close . . . they touch. Contact is a vital condition for life.

* * * *

Without contact, we die. Thus, the more alive, the better we are at making contact with life. This contact is two-sided: letting life pass through us while protecting it so that it can continue its journey. "Whatever has the nature to arise will also pass away."[70]

This acknowledgement is where an affirmative philosophy and mindfulness intersect. As a mindfulness teacher said, "we experience the truth of selflessness when we see nothing last long enough to be called 'self'. All phenomena arise out of appropriate causes and conditions, unsubstantial, empty of any inherent self-existence."[71]

The self is an ongoing process of becoming . . . becoming full of life.

Mindfulness is a practical way of trying to experience that whatever arises will also pass away. This is pure physics. Whether I turn inward, I will notice that I arise and pass away; whether I look out, I will notice that people, tries, norms, and ideas arise and pass. Our responsibility as human beings is always placed in this interval between *no longer* and *not yet,* it is a way of welcoming what is never ours to give: life.

The opposite of mindfulness is being mindless: Being careless with life as it passes us, because we are too pre-occupied or distracted with what happened in the past or what might happen in the future. Absentmindedness or mind wandering are often used as suitable antonyms for mindfulness; daydreaming is another example.

Experiencing what arises and passes or what is not allowed to arise—for example, due to oppression or exploitation—opens for our involvement. Affirmation is a constitutive conception of practice as a foundation of a metaphysic of becoming, which refuses any deep or hidden foundation of being. It's a process that is both destructive and constructive. To free ourselves, we must destroy the dialectical assumption saying that a predefined order is available. This is where a metaphysic of being not only narrows but also blocks our creativity. A metaphysic of becoming—understood as a research project or an unverifiable premise—is the only starting point for making the constitution of being possible.

Deciding what to destroy and what to bring into life, for obvious reasons, requires scrutiny. The psychologist Viktor Frankl said, "Between stimulus and response there is a space. In that space is our power to choose our response. In our response lies our growth and our freedom." By enhancing or widening the space between a stimuli and my response, I hinder an automatic reaction. I hinder following ideological fantasies. I become aware of my limitations, which matures me.

What seems to be the stabilizing factor in a philosophy of mindfulness is the approach. Continuously become other while, at the same time, you remain accountable for what or who you were.

Mindfulness can facilitate more wise responses instead of pure reaction. I suggest that it can qualify and help us scrutinize before we decide. "Do you desire this once more and innumerable times more?" Yes or no? "Whatever you will, will it in such a way that you also will its eternal return." Do you want to kiss her again tomorrow? If your answer is no, then think again.

To act responsibly is to overcome our passivity as well as blindly feeding our starving egos. How may I respond in a way that is beneficial for life? Such a responsibility is disastrous; as Blanchot says, "responsibility that never lightens the Other's burden . . . if it is true that the life of the other is that which must be welcomed by the gift of the ultimate, the gift of that which (in the body and through the body) is not - mine - to give."[72]

What is not mine to give? Life. I must give my life to pass on life.

THERE ARE ONLY LINES

9

MINDFULNESS IS CALLED THE HEART OF BUD-dhism, the Buddhist practice; however, befo-re we explore the heart, we need to have a basic under-standing of the rest of the body. It was not until the 20th century, in particular the last quarter, that mindfulness began to dominate Western interest in Buddhism; before then, the interest was more centered on Buddhism as a belief system, its ethics, and, most notably, the stories of the historical Buddha.

Buddhism refers to a broad and complex religi-ous as well as philosophical tradition. "'Buddhism' is so-mething of an intellectual abstraction: in reality there is no Buddhism but many Buddhisms."[73] In *The Spirit of Buddhist Meditation*, Sarah Shaw writes, "One of the gre-atest strengths of Buddhism is that it lacks a centralized authority and even a single body of core text, containing many in a number of different languages in various regi-ons."[74] Buddhism is not one but many. "Buddha's tree itself becomes a rhizome," wrote Deleuze and Guattari.[75] Any point of a rhizome "can be connected to anything other, and must be . . . There are no points or positions in a rhizome, such as those found in a structure, tree, or root. There are only lines."

Some of these lines intersect with Deleuze's philosophy, whereas some of them seem to point in the opposite direction. In Buddhism, you ascend the mountain of life to reach enlightenment or nirvana. Nirvana is the state of the cessation of all suffering and rebirth. Deleuze may not be a mountaineer, he may not know where he is heading (regarding how he should live his life before he actually lives it); yet, he shares the Buddhist premise that change, renewal, and transformation emerge due to our encounters with life because life is changing.

The overall framework of Buddhism is closer to Plato than Deleuze. The idea of nirvana serves as a moral motivation to escape what is condemned—for example, suffering due to attachment or ignorance. A philosophy of mindfulness is motivated by life itself, not a guiding idea. In philosophy, wisdom gradually emerges by ongoing questioning of our ignorance, and for that reason, we always philosophize on the border of our previous knowledge. You can make your life more joyous as you mature and become less ignorant. Insight transforms your form of living.

* * * *

Both Eastern and Western philosophies begin with an experience of being lost or alienated in life. To philosophize, not just think, is a healing activity. It's a way of getting acquainted and becoming challenged. Wittgenstein said, "A philosophical problem has the form: 'I don't know my way about.'"[76] Perhaps this feeling of being lost is why philosophy begins with a dialogue. It's like asking a good friend for directions, a way of befriending the wise. Yet, whereas the Buddha tells us to seek the truth within, the philosopher encourages us to find our way in a more outgoing fashion.

Plato's dialogues describe Socrates' conversation with his fellow Athenians as he was trying to harmonize their lives—basically, convincing people that wisdom emerges as we acknowledge our ignorance. Philosophy is a dance between knowing and deceiving yourself. The clarifying or illuminating questions emerge from this ignorance. Similarly, the Buddha didn't write down his teaching; he passed it on verbally. Knowledge has always been something that people produce and share in communities. However, what is interesting about both Plato's dialogues and the sutra of

Buddha is that they invite the participator—or, nowadays, the readers—to pass them on, not to necessarily interpret them but to experiment with them . . . test them. You can't read Plato—at least I can't—without asking and exploring what justice, love, or reality is, just as you can't hear that life is suffering without exploring this premise.

Perhaps the students of Socrates, Plato, the Buddha, and other wise men and women have exaggerated the words of their masters, trying to make them wiser. It doesn't matter. They wrote their teachings down out of love. We, today, are formed by the past's generosity and, I believe, we have a responsibility to challenge these ideas and thoughts . . . to think on them so that we, too, can pass forms of life onto future generations so that they might find them inspirational and helpful in their paths toward a freer, more peaceful, and wiser life, leading to a happy and peaceful death.

Reading philosophy is an investigation of yourself; for example, your illusions, delusions, knowledge, ignorance, etc. are being questioned. This is also what brings philosophy to art and art to philosophy—the truths in life always have to be created. For example, it could be the creation of a new lifeline that you can follow.

My first experience with Buddhism came through martial arts and literature in my teens. Jack Kerouac's *The*

Dharma Bums presents Buddhism as an attractive and creative form of life that rebels against the consumerism of capitalism: " . . . Dharma Bums refusing to subscribe to the general demand that they consume production and therefore have to work for the privilege of consuming, all that crap they didn't really want anyway such as refrigerators, TV sets, cars, at least new fancy cars, certain hair oils and deodorants and general junk you finally always see a week later in the garbage anyway, all of them imprisoned in a system of work, produce, consume, work, produce, consume, I see a vision of a great rucksack revolution thousands or even millions of young Americans wandering around with rucksacks, going up the mountain to pray . . . "

Similarly, Buddhism inspired John Cage's composition *4'33"*, which is four minutes and 33 seconds of silence—or almost silence because there is always someone coughing, the movement of bodies, the noise of the wind, or our own breath. The artist Ken Dewey's *Street Pieces*, or happenings, activate certain processes that wake people up. To walk on the street can be both a meaningful and beautiful act, depending on your awareness or attention. Art is a bodily experience. Happenings often make the participators conscious of walking, dancing, or cooking like an actor becomes conscious of acting. You know you are here. Writers and artists were already preparing or setting the scene for mindfulness, as most of us know it today.

* * * *

"Let's go back to the beginning: to the awakening of Siddhartha Gautama, aka the Tathagata, Shakyamuni, the World Honored One—the Buddha himself. He was the one who set the wheel of dharma spinning in the first place."[77] The awakening? The Buddha? The wheel of dharma?

The word *Buddha* is a title, not a name. Similarly, one could say that the word *philosopher* is a title, not a name. The history of Western philosophy is full of different names of philosophers who have contributed ideas, concepts, thoughts, and approaches to life. The word philosopher refers to the friend of wisdom . . . the one who loves wisdom. The word Buddha means "one who has woken up" or "the awakened one." It signifies that such a person experiences what is real.

The Buddha is the title of a historical person, Siddhartha Gautama, who lived approximately 2,500 years ago in what today is known as the north of India and Nepal. Siddhartha Gautama was a prince and, like most princes, he lived a privileged life in his palace, isolated from the worries, pain, and dissatisfaction that affect many other people's lives. One day, the prince left his royal cradle and then, something happened. This is how Buddhism begins: like a classical process of development, almost like a fairytale.

He left a world of wealth, possessions, decadence, and ease of living and entered one of suffering. The awakening of Siddhartha Gautama, therefore, begins with an everyday experience. He experienced things that he could not grasp: hunger, sickness, death, loss, fear, etc., perhaps even stress! Instead of running back to the comfortable life in his palace, Siddhartha Gautama confronted the suffering to see whether it was possible to overcome it. Again, this process is quite well known for most people. We leave the comfortable and safe embrace of our parents (if we are so lucky to have them), and gradually, we are able to interact with life more independently without running back to our parents every two hours. We encounter various setbacks and we hope to become better at handling these due to our formation. Some people seem to have the will to power—the will to invent a path through life, learning from what they encounter—while some resign and victimize themselves, and others look for help or inspiration elsewhere—for example, in Buddhism.

Before Siddhartha Gautama sat down and was enlightened, he asked himself (at least he may have), "Which experience is real?" Is the prince's experience of living in the castle less real than life outside? Of course not. There is only one world; however, he had only experienced a little of what life had to offer. The prince became, for some, a savior and, for others, a scientist, but for all, he became the Buddha. He woke up and saw life for what it really is. At least he experienced a richer, more complex, and more challenging form of living. If Buddhism emphasizes one simple point, it is that reality matters.

Is this really happening, or is it a dream or an illusion? It's because we can't make the distinction that we suffer. Thus, regardless of the wisdom of the Buddha, we should still investigate these claims (the Buddha even encourages his followers to do so). Without an ongoing social and psychological investigation, postulates that are too rigid about what is real can lead directly to a "will to truth" or a "will to good" or a "will of God," whereby we enter a normative setting full of illusions.

* * * *

The question "Which experience is real?" addresses a fundamental philosophical problem. Western philosophy begins with a metaphysical bifurcation that still forms, organizes, and challenges philosophical thought to the present day. Heraclitus, a pre-Socratic philosopher, emphasized the primacy of a changeable and emergent world, whereas Parmenides, his successor, claimed that the nature of reality was permanent and unchangeable. Plato would later follow in the tradition of Parmenides, but was always emphasizing reason and not the mythology of the gods. Philosophy meant the endeavor to understand everything. Free from religion, the philosopher used his or her freedom to think. The two competing traditions— Heraclitus and Parmenides—may be seen as an equivalent to the two competing traditions within Buddhism and Hinduism. In Buddhism, the concept *anatta,* literally non-self, refers to the lack of a permanent self (i.e., the third of the three marks of existence in Buddhism). One example is *Milinda's Questions,* a dialogue between Greek-born king Menander (Milinda) and the sage Nagasena. The sage describes how a wagon consists of wheels, axels, strings, and so on, as an example of how the wagon is an assemblage of various parts; however, one can change these parts and yet still be speaking about the same wagon. Thus, the term "wagon," like "self," is a concept, although an ideal wagon or self doesn't exist. In reality, we could change all parts of the wagon and still speak of it. This view represents the opposite to an even older story from Hinduism that refers to the concept *atman*, literally inner self or soul, which is understood as something permanent behind the various changes of circumstance. Thus, in Hinduism, it's believed that there is a self or soul in all being, whereas in Buddhism, nothing is permanent.

We may call it enlightenment, although the Buddha didn't experience anything other than an alternative to an existing position. This, however, does not make it less interesting, it simply illustrates that Buddhism is part of a shared culture where we test each other's findings. It should be treated like that—not something infallible.

In Western philosophical terms, a *reductionist* understanding claims that there is no essence or principle that the words "I" or "me" refer to, which mean that "I" is used as a way of speaking about something else, for example, skills, characteristics, etc. In addition, and this is my use in this book, it is used as an intersection or encounter of forces or different forms of life. The self is a process of change. Contrary to this exists a *non-reductionist* understanding that claims the existence of something permanent in the human being—for example, consciousness, self, I, subject, etc. The point here is that the "self" or "I" can't be reduced to something else, despite all the changes it undergoes from birth to death.

Thus, even though many people may have a common-sense feeling that there is something deeper inside them, something that lasts or can be recognized over time, it's not because a "self" or "essence" really exists; rather, it is because the change happens gradually or so slowly that we don't even notice it. Furthermore, many cling to the stimulating illusion of being the driver of their own thoughts, feelings, and experiences. The person in the mirror looks like the man I saw yesterday, but he doesn't look like the person I saw ten years ago. A mirror is more than what it reflects: you don't study your reflection in a mirror to know yourself. In addition, some may not notice these differences because we tend to hang onto certain stories about ourselves that we like and wish to be identified by—for example, certain roles, positions, or statuses that such an identity represents within a given society. We seduce our own self into permanent existence for narrative reasons. We thus forget that "Man is something that shall be overcome," as Nietzsche said; that is to say, we transgress our "self."

The human being is not an autonomous agent; rather, we are constantly blended, mixed, or coevolving with other forms of life. The human life is one form of life in between plants, animals, and even machines, which all affect and change one another. Life is a flux of energy or forces where things are broken, then rebroken, and made into something else before they break again.

10

ONCE SIDDHARTHA GAUTAMA BECAME THE BUDDHA, he shared his findings, which later became known as his teachings or *the dharma*. The dharma "is a huge umbrella term with many different meanings. Among others, it means the truths of the way things are. It means the specific elements of experience and the natural laws that govern that experience. *Dharma* also refers to the teaching of the Buddha and to the paths of practice that leads to awakening."[78]

The wheel of the dharma can serve as a useful metaphor. Whoever invented the wheel made it possible and easier, back then and today, to carry heavy things and even to carry things that you couldn't otherwise lift. The teachings of Buddha also help people carry many of life's burdens, despite the nausea, despair, meaninglessness, or suffering that we all at times experience. The wheel can help you to move on. The wheel will not change the weight—twenty kilos are still twenty kilos, just as one dead brother is still one dead brother—but it may feel lighter. It is bearable. Buddhism (and mindfulness) shares some of the attitudes that you can find in philosophical existentialism—for example, if life really is like the myth of Sisyphus rolling the same rock up the hill only to see it fall down, then what is the value? The value lies in the fact that you're actually not repeating the same thing over and over; the value is in the differences that each day consists of. The practice of pushing up the rock brings you in contact with life, with history, with other people. Someone before you was probably trying to push the same rock up the hill, just as you may not succeed and someone else will take over. These small differences and connections can help you appreciate living a life that—at least for the majority of us—appears to be more or less the same every day.

How to move on despite the absurdities? One answer lies in paying attention to the difference, the interdependence of it all, regardless of how small the differences seem or how fragile the relations are. Paying attention is connected to acknowledging or accepting our vulnerability. New experiences are often born out of wounds or painful experiences; we progress as we learn to live with them.

* * * *

Buddhism can be summarized in the band The The's lovely song "Lonely Planet," where it says, "If you can't change the world, change yourself." Instead of changing the world, it's easier, or perhaps more realistic at least, to change *your* world—that is, to change how you perceive and live with the world. How is your relationship with the world? In reality, you're not changing yourself according to some shiny ideal; rather, you recognize your own patterns of behavior. Learn from experience. Act in concordance with life, not against it. Let go of what's keeping you nailed to the ground. Braidotti says, "When you remember to become what you are—a subject-in-becoming—you actually reinvent yourself on the basis of what you hope you could become with a little help from your friends."[79]

The lyrical statements of The The, of course, always carry the risk of trivializing something difficult and honorable. Still, changing your relationship with life is not necessarily easy, even if you're motivated. The majority of us have the habit of following habits, including those that are not so beneficial. In addition, another problem, as mentioned earlier, is what we do if the world remains the same although we have changed. For example, we live in a competitive world that forces us to achieve and perform in relation to capitalistic values; here, my time with crossed legs isn't helping much, although it's a beginning. In other words, structures also need to be changed on a systemic level by the decision makers. However, instead of referring to a better illusion world, I advocate for a change within— utopia as a "now here," not a nowhere. In addition, it is important to recognize that the "processes of becoming are collective, intersubjective, and not individual or isolated."[80] Even Buddhist monks who live isolated are not alone; they are part of a culture that changes.

* * * *

Buddhism emphasizes that your potential progress toward enlightenment depends on how you're changing yourself—especially changing your mind. However, many things can make a person's mind change: meditation, sickness, love, drugs, or alcohol. Some of these changes are more beneficial or healthy than others; it is here that Buddhism serves as a moral motivator.

In alignment, Mahatma Gandhi is much celebrated for the statement, "Be the change you wish to see in the world." Said by him (regardless of whether he really did say it), it becomes a powerful and inspiring statement. It makes sense because of the form of life that he practiced. However, if a psychopath, fascist, racist, or patriarch had said it, this statement would no longer make sense. In alignment with Buddhism and Hinduism, as well as Tolstoy and Thoreau, Gandhi emphasized how nonviolence served as the positive intent behind his action: "The final test as to [whether it is violent or non-violent] is after all the intent underlying the act."[81] For Gandhi, nonviolence was not the same as not acting; rather, it was a nonviolent action. Nonviolence became both a guiding idea and a strategy.

In other words, you shouldn't just follow your heart because most of us—at least until we become wiser and more mature—have wanted things that were not good for us. Instead, we should cultivate our hearts based on what is really important and valuable in life. By protecting and caring for life, I don't refer to my life as such but the life that passes through me and allows me to be the same—that is, the other.

I mention "the heart" because it is filled with symbolic power that can be used to defend even selfish actions, as when people deliberately violate other human beings by saying, "I was just following my heart." Here, we excuse our ignorance behind our heart, which still makes us ignorant and, therefore, careless. Of course, the heart signifies (metaphorically) our emotional balance, whereto we may ask whether certain emotions really are good for us, or if they are signs of us being unaware.

Cultivation is a continual awareness of the passage of being conscious in relation to what happens and how this affects us. It bears witness to our experience of interaction with life; it's an ongoing evaluation that takes place while we live. No one can become wise without mingling with life, trying and failing, and so forth. This, furthermore, touches upon Aristotle's dilemma of being good, because you would have to know what is good in order to be so, but you can only know what is good if you have experienced it. A useful guide is, however, your state of mind. For example, you should only engage yourself out of interest, curiosity, admiration, or care, and not out of hate, greed, or envy.

* * * *

The dharma can be seen as a helping tool—a tool that still spins today, just like the wheel is used for carriages, bikes, or Formula 1 cars. The wheel emphasizes something important, which is that time is folded; the past is with us today, and it is probably also part of what is coming. We can't separate the past, present, and future; rather, they constantly fertilize one another. Bikes, cars, and carriages change, but something remains the same: the wheel.

Similarly, life has always been difficult and full of suffering, pain, or heavy burdens. The kinds of difficulties, suffering, or pain may have changed drastically, although some may be more or less the same—for example, a broken heart. Still, there is one tool—although not the only tool—that has helped people since Siddhartha Gautama sat on the Bodhi spot where he obtained enlightenment: the wheel of dharma. Sadly, perhaps, it seems like this wheel is more needed than ever in our contemporary capitalist performance society. We have lost our place in and with life.

The dharma outlines a path—a natural law seen from a Buddhist perspective—that leads to awakening or enlightenment. Although there are disagreements about some points of the dharma, one formulation remains central to all: the *Four Noble Truths*.

11

THE FOUNDATION OF THE BUDDHA'S TEACHING IS KNOWN as the Four Noble Truths. These truths are not noble because the Buddha was nobility. Rather, when a person matures and gains wisdom, we may say that his or her spirit is noble, just as Plato suggested that "the Good" was beautiful and just.

The Four Noble Truths are:

1. The features of life, which exemplify suffering (or pain)

2. The causes of suffering

3. The reality that can lead to the cessation of suffering

4. The path leading to liberation from suffering

Suffering is an integrated part of life for the Buddhist. Every time there is life, there is suffering. Suffering is the typical English translation of the word *dukka,* which also refers to "frustration," "difficulty," "limitation," "bad-ness," or the "image of an axle not fitting properly into its hole."[82] These etymological understandings give associations to concepts such as imbalance or disharmony; basically, you're suffering because you're not attuned with the rhythm of life. You're lost. Disconnected. Alienated.

According to Buddhism, there are eight types of suffering for humans: birth, aging, sickness, death, losing friends, making enemies, not finding what you want (i.e., desire), and finding what you do not want (i.e., aversion). One kind of suffering that the Buddhist does not operate with explicitly is solitude, the existential condition of life from which empathy and compassion emerge. Camus spoke of a division between himself and the rest of the humans as a painful condition that we all share.

The Buddhist operates with the suffering of pain (e.g., the previous eight forms of suffering), the suffering of change (e.g., how pleasure at one point turns into pain), and the suffering of conditioning. The last, the suffering of conditioning, is related to the underlying principle of the dharma—that is, life is conditioned by causes and events that the human being can't control. The existential problem emerges because some people don't understand, or accept, that pleasure is a form of pain and that pain can appear at any moment. You never know which beer is going to be the last before you get sick. Even Romeo and Juliet were doomed from the beginning, not just because of the disagreement between their families, but qua being mortals, their love story had to end one day. Of course, due to Shakespeare's genius, it ended in a very affective way.

Life is suffering. The writer Thomas Ligotti writes, "*Buddhism is pessimism.*"[83] He goes on to claim that we feel " . . . shortchanged if there is nothing else for us than to survive, reproduce, and die. We want there to be more to it than that, or to think there is. This is a tragedy." It is. The tragedy is, however, where the pessimist and the Buddhist part.

The Buddhist believes that you can find happiness if you follow the teachings of the Buddha; the pessimist doesn't share such a belief. So, for the Buddhist, it may be seen as a tragedy that the pessimist deprives himself or herself of the opportunity of experiencing a higher form of being—state of mind—where you become more developed or mature, even happy. For the pessimist, the Buddhist truths and learnings are just another set of illusions, and not examples of matureness.

Pessimism, tragedy, suffering, what is it?

I don't see it as black and white as Ligotti, although I welcome his bluntness. For example, "the sangha"—association or community of mindfulness meditators—may be a helpful reminder for the practitioners, for example, keeping focused on your path, sharing experiences. And still we need to be cautious regarding the risk that the sangha doesn't turn into an example of "groupthink," where the security, comfort, and desired harmony of the group results in irrational decisions, for instance, when every critical viewpoint is being suppressed.

It makes Buddhism less receptive and less open if Buddhists want everything to fit the picture of the reality that the Buddha experienced. I assume this is why the Buddha—some of its teachers—always encourages questioning his findings, or as one Zen quote famously says, "If you meet the Buddha, kill the Buddha. If you meet the Ghost, kill the Ghost." This emphasizes several things: First of all, that you should not become blindly attached to your teacher. In addition, a good teacher is actually the one who sets you free . . . the one you don't need any more at some point. Furthermore, you should only kill the Buddha as a concept, an idealized construct of the mind that blurs your own experiences and hinders you from thinking freely.

To think is to explore the limits of our knowledge. So, think of the Buddha until he can no longer be an object, because then you cannot identify with him. It's a state of mind. I encourage people to experiment, but always with the knowledge that infallible gurus only exist in religion. Diversity is a celebration of the many different and creative forms that a life takes.

Is it the faith in the Buddha's teachings that brings peace of mind, or is it the quest of trying to understand what is this thing called life?

12

We suffer due to our ignorant mind. The second truth suggests that we suffer because we desire what we do not have, or we suffer from aversion because we do not want or like what we have, or we suffer because we are ignorant of how everything is interdependent. Ignorance is the main enemy of enlightenment and wisdom. The truth, therefore, is a cultivation of our well-being as a way of getting rid of our ignorance.

The third truth deals mainly with becoming aware of a thought or a feeling, rather than being lost in a thought or identifying with a feeling. That is, becoming aware of the real world, not some fantasy or delusion. This awareness is being mindful. It is within this third truth that a whole industry of well-being has emerged. The self-help industry is growing to the extent that it makes you wonder if some indecent consultants are making people suffer just to sell them a cure.

The fourth truth proposes a path toward liberation

from all suffering. Mindfulness is an example of a practice that has gained huge popularity because it can put an end to concrete suffering, such as stress, anxiety, obesity, etc. To a large extent, mindfulness has been a revolution, an act of rebellion—that is, non-doing in a time obsessed with performance. Mindfulness resembles Melville's *Bartleby, the Scrivener: A Story of Wall Street,* where Bartleby refuses to do any of the assignments required of him, with the words "I prefer not to."

Although suffering rarely is appreciated, I wonder whether a life without any kind of wounds is attractive. Learning is, to a large extent, a painful experience because it is painful to be confronted with your ignorance. When we encounter something that violates the harmony we experience, we are forced to think, to reevaluate, and to change. Our habits get a knockout. Here, pain is a part of maturing and acknowledging our limitations or failures.

In *Refuge,* Williams says, "Buddha says there are two kinds of suffering: the kind that leads to more suffering and the kind that brings an end to suffering."[84] This could suggest that the philosophical pain that I mention only illustrates that I am not yet as illuminated as the Buddha is. It also illustrates that philosophical wisdom is never given.

Yet, it is funny (not wrong or false) that these Buddhist arguments are that they are the exact opposite of what Aristotle would consider "excellence in character." For Aristotle, excellence in character is not illustrated by the ex-smoker who no longer smokes a pack a day—the one who suffers—but by the person who never took up an addiction. Excellence in character is shown in a person who effortlessly acts as he or she wants; for example, the ex-smoker shows strength of will, not excellence in character. The underlying moral is to both want and will what you do—that is, to act or live in a way that your thoughts, feelings, and acts are in harmony.

Most people who find inspiration or help in mindfulness or other philosophies begin their practice due to strength of character—his or her will—that gradually transforms into excellence in character.

I might be wrong, but not even Plato or Aristotle were born the wise men that we know them to be today.

* * * *

The four truths serve as an undisputable axiom for Buddhist practice, partly so in mindfulness, regardless of whether mindfulness is practiced in a Buddhist or non-Buddhist context. Although everything changes, these truths are unchangeable. Is this a paradox? Perhaps, but it brings Buddhism and Deleuze both closer and further away, as I have already shown.

Now, against this background, let's ask: What are the differences between Buddhism and Deleuze? For Deleuze, there are no fixed points, no claims that life *is* suffering. Instead life is difference. Therefore, he would not say that life is suffering, nor what is the origin of suffering; rather, he proposes that philosophy is to set out new coordinates or produce new lines for the practice of thinking—that is, thinking freely as something other than representation or reflection. This doesn't mean that there is not suffering in life. It's obvious there is, but there is also joy. Just take a look at any playground. Here you can witness children full of joy because they are alive. Furthermore, Buddhism suggests that there is a path. Deleuze rejects the teleology of enlightenment; a philosopher doesn't follow tracks. For me, this makes philosophy liberating. The philosopher philosophizes without a compass.

Thus, in general, Buddhism *partly* resembles Platonism (there is a different joyous taste for life in Plato; he would also call into question whether life really is suffering). Yet, I am aware of the pragmatic approach that especially mindfulness exhibits. For example, you can see the four truths as a diagnostic scheme:

1. Symptom = dissatisfaction

2. Cause = craving

3. Prognosis = ending dissatisfaction

4. Treatment = the Eightfold Path

The challenge is, of course, whether the Buddha doctor wants to explain why you have the symptoms that you have, or whether the doctor wants to understand. Although one doesn't necessarily exclude the other, it often does. The question is whether sense is given or produced, or whether you seek to make a specific sense out of something because it fits with your medicaments. Hereby, Buddhism also resembles the German philosopher Kant since he makes the good (e.g., nirvana) revolve around the law (i.e., the dharma and karma). "In Plato, laws were secondary or derived power, subordinate to the Good; if humans knew the Good, and how to conform to it, they would not need laws."[85] For the Buddha, the Four Noble Truths serve as the law—a necessary law because people don't know the good. Kant turns this around when he makes the law primary. Deleuze tried to overcome this battle between the good or the law through Nietzsche and Spinoza, for example, questioning the very principles of the moral law. *Who* is it that says, "You must!"—"You should!"

It may also be here, I propose, that mindfulness

distinguishes itself from Buddhism because the law judges life from a higher position (i.e., enlightenment), whereas mindfulness is a nonjudgmental practice.

The Four Noble Truths relate to the Noble Eightfold Path. This is one way that can help one overcome the suffering of life. The link between the truths and the path follows Wittgenstein's skeptical view of truth—Wittgenstein's ironies over how we perceive the truth. "One must start out with error and convert it into truth."[86] The error is that life is suffering. "That is, one must reveal the source of error, otherwise hearing the truth won't do any good. The truth can't force its way in when something else is occupying its place." Desire, aversion, craving, and ignorance are the sources of this error. The point is that you can only claim that certain causes lead to certain effects within a particular language game or mutual understanding, for example, that life is suffering. To put it differently, if you're convinced that the picture you have about the world is true, this understanding then affects how you live. My objection is that having a clear picture of the truth makes your approach to life less open, less flexible; in philosophy, means and ends are unknown. For the Buddhist, they are not. Therefore, as Wittgenstein says, "To convince someone of the truth, it is not enough to state it, but rather one must find the *path* from error to truth."

The Buddhist calls this path the Noble Eightfold Path.

13

THE NOBLE EIGHTFOLD PATH CONSISTS OF THE FOLLOW-ing guidelines:[87]

1. Balanced or right view, i.e., seeing the four truths

2. Balanced or right intention, i.e., desirelessness, friendliness, and compassion

3. Balanced or right speech, i.e., refraining from false, divisive, and hurtful speech, as well as idle chatter

4. Balanced or right action, i.e., refraining from harming living beings, from taking what is not given, and from sexual misconduct

5. Balanced or right livelihood, i.e., not based on wrong speech and action

6. Balanced or right effort, i.e., to prevent unarisen unwholesome states, to abandon arisen unwholesome states, to arouse unarisen wholesome states, and to develop arisen wholesome states

7. Balanced or right mindfulness, i.e., contemplation

of body, feeling, mind, and dharma

8. Balanced or right concentration, i.e., practice of the four dhyánas (meditation or perfect mental calmness and equilibrium)

The Noble Eightfold Path consists of three forms of training: wisdom, conduct (or ethics), and meditation (concentration and observation). Wisdom refers to the "balanced view" and the "balanced intention." Conduct refers to the "balanced speech," the "balanced action," and the "balanced livelihood." Meditation refers to the remainder: the "balanced effort," the "balanced mindfulness," and the "balanced concentration." Some only use the word "right" in the context of the Noble Eightfold Path, whereas others stress that the word "right" makes you assume that there is one correct way that one *should* or *ought* to follow; words such as *should*, *ought*, and *must* are limiting and inflexible. Balance, on the other hand, is a more dynamic concept. It depends on the circumstances. Furthermore, balance incorporates both body and mind as when we change our body positions due to the surface. How I respond depends on my capacity to empathically understand those people's lives that I am affected by, understand the conditions that affect them in a certain way. Balance respects how things are connected.

Similarly, if I mistreat nature, I am also mistreating myself. Looking at the world today, it is obvious that many people don't feel connected with nature, other people, or different forms of life; instead, many seem to separate themselves as a way of protecting what they believe to be theirs. This form of protective thinking is related to ideological thinking—for instance, nationalism or capitalism with its idea of the relationship between possession and freedom—whereas what I suggest is that possessions only break the flow of life and make us less agile. In other words, nature is not something "out there"; it is an intimate part us.

In addition, the word balance has been one of ethics' most central concepts since Aristotle's concept of the Golden Mean as the appropriate way between two extremes—for example, between joy and sadness, courage or cowardice, etc. Similarly, the Eightfold Path is a middle way between various extremes.

The middle way in Buddhism describes the path between being and non-being, desire and aversion, and form and emptiness. It aims at equanimity, which is part of the Seven Factors of Enlightenment in Buddhism (i.e., calm, concentration, rapture [or joy], equanimity, mindfulness, energy, and investigations). Equanimity refers to balance and harmony. "The middle lies at the heart of the meditative practice."[88] Equanimity is not indifference or passivity. It emphasizes how balance is *balancing*.

Spiritual maturity consists of several qualities; one of these is "non-idealism." "The mature heart is not perfectionistic: it rests in the compassion of our being instead of in ideals of the mind."[89] Finding balance is an intuitive process of sense making—finding and creating our way through life. To live an ethical life is to live a form of life in balance understood as something dynamic.

* * * *

Buddhism and mindfulness are ways of training your balancing skills. Especially in many of the different approaches to mindfulness, balancing becomes both a mental and bodily skill—for example, as training in yoga or martial art. Depending on the teachers, you may either train in all skills at the same time or follow a phased progress. For example, according to Gethin, "the three aspects of the practice of the path exist [i.e., wisdom, conduct and meditation], operate, and are developed in a mutually dependent and reciprocal relationship."[90] Another Buddhist scholar and teacher suggests that wisdom seems to be the result of good conduct and concentration. "First we train in morality, in nonharming. If we try to practice meditation without the foundation of goodwill to ourselves and others, it is like trying to row across a river without first untying the boat; our effort, no matter how strenuous, will not bear fruit. We need to practice and refine our ability to live honestly and with integrity. In the second training, we develop energy, concentration, and mindfulness. These are the meditative and life tools that enable us to awaken. Without them we simply act out the patterns of our conditioning. These two trainings are the foundation for the third, which is the emergence of wisdom. Wisdom is the clear seeing of the impermanent, conditioned nature of all phenomena, knowing that whatever arises has the nature to cease. When we see this impermanence deeply, we no longer cling; and when we no longer cling, we come to the end of suffering."[91]

Perhaps the order is not that important. Instead conduct, meditation, and wisdom can be seen as a three-legged stool. This is also what makes the practice temporary since your level of stability is constantly present. Mindfulness typically operates with two kinds of meditations that the Buddha taught: *samatha* and *vipassana*. Samatha is a single-pointed meditation that aims at calming the mind, for example, through mindfulness of your breathing. It cultivates a clear comprehension or concentration. The breath becomes the anchor that you gently return to once you discover that your mind is drifting. Vipassana refers to a clear vision or insight (e.g., insight meditation). To put it simply, when mindfulness is used in stress reduction, a major part of the practice helps people relax, and then they can concentrate, observe, and perhaps gain insight of various kinds. This process of gaining insight, I propose, is not only inward as it also makes you aware of your relationship with the world, how it affects you, and how you affect it. This may help you make wiser decisions.

* * * *

In Buddhism, the thesis is that each one of us is or incorporates all previous beings that lived before us. The process toward enlightenment is, therefore, a detoxification. "Wisdom, great king, when it arises, dispels the darkness of ignorance, produces the brilliance of clear knowledge, makes the light of understanding (ñánaloka) appear, and makes the noble truths easy to discern. And the practitioner then knows impermanence, suffering and non-self with right wisdom."[92]

We need to get rid of all the toxic emotions or thoughts that pollute our minds, such as desire, attachment, anger, forgetfulness, distractions, greed, jealousy, etc., as well as all the toxic emotions and thoughts that previous consciousness has passed on to us. For this reason, creation and destruction fold around one another. If you are to reach nirvana—a state without greed and desire—you actually need to destroy the mind and body. Nirvana is enlightenment free from rebirth. "There can be no mind and body because there is no karma to cause them . . . Among the many wisdoms of the Buddha, there is a famous pair: the knowledge that ignorance has been destroyed and the knowledge that it will never be produced again."[93] This is to reach nothingness.

The nature of emptiness is where the void is empty. It is also the point where there is no reincarnation because the human race is extinct. Of course, since there is not a self in Buddhism, it is not the self that reincarnates, but what was sustainable in a person's actions.

It may sound scary—non-self, suffering, and impermanence—because it requires courage to leave a comfortable zone of illusionary stability. Yet, it is also a pragmatic truth emphasizing "what is better for us to believe," rather than "the accurate representation of reality is simply an automatic and empty compliment which we pay to those beliefs which are successful in helping us do what we want to do."[94] For example, overcoming difficult stages in our lives by improving our self-image is an example of such empty compliments because we find it too difficult or sad to accept that we don't own our selves.

Meditation can be a powerful tool to clean your mind . . . not emptying it but being aware of what is going on right now and then deciding: Do you want to cultivate it? Should you let it go? Do you want to cultivate vanity?

The crucial question is, of course, who decides and how to decide. Is it the law? Is it the truth? Or does it depend on how things work due to our experiments with what comes into being? Once you pay attention without an agenda, you also experience that you're not your thoughts or feelings. They belong to no one. They are a part of the relation that you have with the world. Instead of saying "I am angry, smart, or powerful," you could say "This is anger . . . " and notice how selflessness comes from being open to everything as well as an acceptance of whatever happens. Through meditation, you can observe the situation where feelings occur and how you identify with them, and then you can gradually learn how to let go of this attachment or change the situation.

* * * *

The philosopher Leibniz once asked, "Why is there something rather than nothing?"

I propose a middle position. There is no thing, only

relations. Things come to life through relationships. For example, the fly only exists for the spider in the moment it touches the web. If we assume that the spider constructed its web to catch the fly, we are adding an abstraction, looking for an "accurate representation" that separates us from the relationship between the spider and the web. "It has no perceptions, no sensations. It responds to signals, nothing else . . . responds to its vibrations."[95]

This example resembles one used by Gethin in *The Foundation of Buddhism*, where he writes, "The mind that is in process is the mind that is actively perceiving objects and reacting to those objects; the mind that is free of process is resting in the inactive mode known as *bhavanga*. This inactive mode characteristically occurs in deep, dreamless sleep. However, according to the theory of consciousness process, the mind momentarily returns to the inactive mode of *bhavanga* between each consciousness process. The mind in this inactive mode of *bhavanga* is compared to a spider resting in the middle of its web. The web extends out in different directions and when one of the threads of the web is struck by an insect the spider in the middle stirs, and then runs out along the thread and bites into the insect to drink its juice."[96]

Did the Four Noble Truths emerge from life?

According to the legend, they did. Still, not to be

polemical or not being grateful and inspired by Buddhist thinking, I favor a friendly confrontation, where you question, explore, and experiment with every position. Such careful scrutinizing is not blindly outlining a new fixed position under the name of being in opposition, rather it is accepting being placed in a continuous pre-position. If, for example, you only feel and think what you have been told to feel and think, then you have not yet experienced what it is to be thought or felt—that is, to be touched by life. This may not contradict Buddhism and mindfulness (less the latter), but it is a delicate balance. "To see the richness of the present moment, we need to cultivate what has been called 'beginner's mind,' a mind that is willing to see everything as if for the first time."[97]

Allowing life to guide you requires an attention to that which cannot be generated from within thought itself. That is to say, we are formed by life; the substance of our thinking depends on what affects us.

A thought, therefore, is not a reflection about something but experimentation with actuality. Meditation can be seen as a kind of experimentation. The experienced meditator Kornfield writes, "no matter what remarkable state arises, we must learn to allow it to come and go freely, recognizing that it is not the goal of meditation . . . we are awakened to the profound realization that the true path to liberation is to *let go of everything,* even the states and fruits of practices themselves, and to open to that which is beyond all identity."[98]

All relations are external to their terms; this is why it is so important that we relate to everything that happens with the same un-strategic openness and care, so we can discover what and how it happens and whether it agrees with us or not. The whole process of perceiving, receiving, and investigating happens very fast. Typically, this is because our present perception is based on our previous ones, determining, for example, whether something is desirable or undesirable, wholesome or unwholesome. Although the basic experiences that a person has are activated by his or her new encounters, they can't be controlled. Yet, "in each consciousness process the mind has a choice in how it will react to the experienced object."[99]

Will you react based on your default setting or autopilot, or will you respond with an open consciousness? Will you respond only to feed your ego?

The particular experience that a person is having right here and now and the future experiences that this person may cultivate right here and now depend on his or her previous karma. The past and the future, therefore, are processes implicated in our living present. Karma means that nothing is free, not in a capitalistic sense, but in a sense that our relationship with life requires hard work and how this relationship affects our experiences.

No one gets away with anything. That is karma. Every morning, you make your bed, and every night you must lie in it.

14

THE DHARMA IS A NATURAL LAW OF CAUSATION. BUD-
DHA's teachings are about those things that have a cause—for example, suffering—and how these causes can
end. The concept of karma emphasizes an intimate relationship between your personal ethics, meditation, and
wisdom. (It's debatable whether a "personal ethics" is possible when everything hangs together).

Karma means "how actions bring results." It can be
seen as being parallel to the old Greek concepts of hubris
and nemesis. For example, if you offend the gods, then the
unavoidable happens: punishment. If you don't live according to the laws of the dharma, then you will suffer.

All our actions related to the Noble Eightfold Path
interact in a dynamic relationship with other forms of life.
This is an ongoing chain of life. Karma, therefore, is an
important Buddhist concept—perhaps the most important because it expresses the principles of the law. Within
Buddhism, it refers to a natural moral law that influences

how we experience life.

"The Buddha identified karma as a volitional activity. That is, each volition in the mind is like a seed with tremendous potential. In the same way that the smallest acorn contains the potential of a great oak tree, so too each of our willed actions contains the seed of karmic results. The particular result depends on the qualities of mind associated with each volition. Greed, hatred, and delusion are unwholesome qualities that produce the fruits of suffering; generosity, love, and wisdom are wholesome factors that bear fruits of happiness."[100]

Greed, hatred, and delusion can also be seen as three basic unconscious forms of the default setting of our mind—that is, our most frequent state of mind: 1) *The desired types*, where your state of mind is associated with grasping and wanting. Here, you just can't get enough. 2) *The aversion types*, where your state of mind is to judge and dislike, even hate. 3) *The confused type*, where your state of mind is disconnected and deluded. Like all models, this, too, reduces the complexity of what it means to be human beings. This, however, doesn't hinder that such typologies can help a person gain self-knowledge, for example, by being aware if he or she is deceiving himself or herself. However, and more importantly, you may notice how a particular approach leads to either a fruitful relationship with the world or closes potential relationships—that is, using these ideal types to reach out. Our repeated mental attitude, our default setting or autopilot, gradually becomes the condition for our personality. Mindfulness helps us to become familiar with our deeper emotional patterns; for example, unhealthy patterns that we need to let go of, the ones that make us care less for what is not me. It helps us to become familiar with something that is just passing by.

The practice resembles, to some extent, the two dictums in Greek philosophy—"Know yourself" and "Take care of yourself"—where the better you become familiar with your approach to life, that is, what you know and don't know, the better you can take care of yourself, and vice versa. For Socrates, self-knowledge was battling with self-deception. Often, we deceive ourselves when we hang on to a certain self-image, or we invent specific self-images for strategic purposes: work, love, and recognition. As Teju Cole illustrates in his novel *Open City*, "I told the story to Nadége on our way back into Manhattan that day. Perhaps she fell in love with the idea of myself that I presented in that story. I was the listener, the compassionate African who paid attention to the details of someone else's life and struggle. I had fallen in love with that idea myself."

We fall in love with our own goodness, our capacity

to make a good story out of our past, present, and future project. At times, it can seem like everyone is constantly dating, trying to present the world with the most seductive version. Another term for this is self-love that resembles selfishness.

Karma doesn't imply that your actions bring about predetermined results. In many ways, we are all powerless regarding what came before us, as well as what will happen after we're gone. This makes sense whether you believe in reincarnation or not. Also, this is the reason why Buddhists and many other philosophers pay attention to the present moment because worrying about what can't be changed or controlled is unproductive, such as the sadness of dwelling and being stuck in the past or the fear and anxiety of focusing too much on the future and what may happen. It doesn't mean that you are not learning from past experiences or that your view of the future is not gradually being qualified (some may call it realistic); rather, it's an intervening time where you experience the flow of time as it moves you right here and now. Each "action is a seed, and the seed will bear some fruit, but what that particular fruit will be depends on many different conditions interacting in extraordinarily subtle and complex ways."[101]

Karma is an ethical concept. It basically emphasizes that how a human being decides to face what he or she encounters affects himself or herself, as well as other people and animals. It affects the planet. As you mature, your knowledge, responsibility, and commitment evolve. The self is never something stable; it is a process formed by your encounters with life. The way each one of us relates to what happens creates our future karma. "The intention that we bring creates the pattern that results."[102]

Even if you're skeptical about the Buddhist idea of reincarnation, most people can still understand the ethical quality related to the idea that our actions leave behind a trace, like the smell of sweat hanging onto our shirts, or a hangover from yesterday's unbalanced drinking.

* * * *

Let us recapitulate. The main difference between Deleuze and Buddhism is, I believe, one of openness. In other words, one of judging, which is also the distinguishing mark between Buddhism and mindfulness in so far as mindfulness is a nonjudgmental practice.

Both try to overcome the prison of having (or being forced) to live up to an identity; yet, the openness I mention refers to our ability to be affected and to affect. Instead of following a moral map, the philosopher is more a cartographer, a mapmaker. Perhaps, the main difference between Deleuze and Buddhism is one of love.

Love is what changes everything.

An example: some spiritual teachers like to claim that we *must* love ourselves before we can love another. To emphasize this point, some mention how an adult, often a parent, is advised to put on his or her seat belt and air mask in a plane before helping his or her child. The moral is "You must love yourself before you can love another." This is an example of egoism, as well as passive nihilism. Nietzsche used the concept "nihilism" to describe the lack of cultural values in his time that could secure a meaningful existence. Nihilism was something to overcome, for example, by producing works of art that bring new existential values and beliefs to the world, or nihilism could be overcome by saying "yes" to life. Just by living life, you actually refute nihilism since it can't be overcome by referring to another transcendent world, ultimate referent, or unchangeable ideals, which Nietzsche would refer to as "passive nihilism."

In passive nihilism, the passivity is related to establishing a sacred position elsewhere (i.e., a state of mind) or referring to another transcendent ideal that operates on a personal level (i.e., my enlightenment). An active approach, on the contrary, opens towards life as such. So, whether mindfulness is an example of active or passive nihilism depends on how it is practiced. If it is self-righteous and only inward turning, then it is passive. Yet, if it is seen solely as an approach or practice—that is, a curious and flexible way of living that may help us in choosing what brings most value to life—then it can be active. To put it simply: mindfulness can play an active role in an affirmative philosophy in so far as it can help us direct society in the best possible way. Merely meditating will not change discriminating social structures, but it can help elucidate the need to do so.

Therefore, when I use mindfulness as an element in an affirmative philosophy, or outlining a philosophy of mindfulness, then I aim at "transcending the negativity itself, transforming it into something positive. This transformation is only possible if one does not sit in judgment either upon oneself or upon others, but rather recognizes within oneself the difficulties involved in not giving into the paranoid-narcissistic self-nexus."[103]

Returning to love, especially the term "self-love", then self-love is nonsense since it involves no *external* cause. Love is, on the other hand, necessarily collective and expansive in the sense that it increases our power to act and hence our joy. It is, therefore, important to distinguish between self-compassion—that is, taking care of yourself—and self-love—that is, an ego trip. Similarly, to feel comfortable in your own skin is not self-love; self-love is a rather absurd concept. It is clinging to an illusion of the authentic self.

The Danish philosopher Søren Kierkegaard wrote in a letter to his fiancé that "freedom is the element of love," stressing that if you are not free to resist all the ideals and norms of contemporary society, you are not capable of loving. If you're not free of polishing your own self-image, then, of course, you can only love yourself. To love is to be formed by the outside; it requires a radical openness to whatever.

Similarly, in Kierkegaard's *Kjerligheden Gjerninger* (*Works on Love*), he shows how the love of the other transcends the logic of desire. I can't mirror myself in the other; rather, he or she is a provocation . . . something extraordinary. This is also why the ones we love are often the biggest strangers in our lives. As Kierkegaard puts it, "Love means to presuppose love; to have love means to presuppose love in others; to be loving means to presuppose that others are loving."[104] Love is something I can experience when I become free.

IT ALWAYS MATTERS

15

MINDFULNESS IS THE MEANS AND THE END . . . the seed and the fruit. As you pay closer attention through concentration, you also become more aware of life, and you experience being alive. [105] You experience how you don't own life. It is something that flows through you and around you. You interact to become alive.

Similar to philosophy, mindfulness is "a way of being . . . It is more akin to wisdom."[106] It enables us to live more fully and more freely. It is a basic human capacity.

During the last decade, there has been an explosive growth of mindfulness in health care, education, business, prisons, the military, and politics. Such growth alone doesn't say anything about mindfulness per se, but it says quite a lot about contemporary society and its need for an alternative approach to life—a more life-affirming approach.

Yet, mindfulness has and is also being used as a business tool for the profitable optimization of the workforce. The problem is not whether mindfulness can or can't facilitate a change in business thinking—non-doing can be seen as rather rebellious— instead, it is how it is practiced. Those who market mindfulness as a coping tool to maintain the pace or as a tool to improve the self-image of the client are doing something else. An important aspect of mindfulness is that everything, including our selves, is a changing process, not a fixed being or essence. Therefore, to practice mindfulness in order to reach a certain self-image or any ideal reduces it to instrumentalism. The problem, therefore, is not mindfulness per se, but rather the business therapists, consultants, and coaches who offer a "quick fix healing."[107]

To put it simply: being mindful can be a wake-up call regarding many of the things that we take for granted. Each experience potentially leads to new questions, which then leads to new knowledge. The point is that knowledge is transformative. The transformation happens with the production of knowledge.

Through meditation, I have learned, as more than an academic abstraction, that as a human being I am intimately linked to other life forms. I am not an independent self. I am full of everything that makes a move on me.

* * * *

Mindfulness is the preferred English translation of the Pali word "sati" (in Sanskrit *smrti*). "Sati is an activity."[108] It is achieved. The word is derived from the root "to remember"; however, it also connotes awareness, attention, and being alert to events occurring in the present whether in the body, the feelings, the mind, or an interplay between all three. Mindfulness is based on these four foundations: awareness of body, feeling, mind, and *dharmas*. The body, feeling, mind, and dharma are also called the four foundations of mindfulness.

In the book, *Mindfulness in Plain English,* written by the Buddhist monk Bhante Henepola Gunaratana, many definitions are expressed: "Mindfulness is presymbolic . . . Mindfulness is the reality that gives rise to words . . . Mindfulness is mirror-thought . . . Mindfulness is nonjudgmental observation . . . Mindfulness is an impartial watchfulness . . . Mindfulness is nonconceptual awareness . . . Mindfulness is present-moment awareness . . . Mindfulness is nonegoistic alertness . . . Mindfulness is awareness of change . . . Mindfulness is participatory observation . . . Mindfulness is a process."[109]

Although these definitions are meant as an introduction to mindfulness, they are quite dense. A few additional words are needed to illustrate how these definitions cohere.

Mindfulness is presymbolic because it deals with experiences that often lie beyond our previous words and symbols. Words are not capable of creating a one-to-one picture of the world. In the beginning, there were no words—only noise. Words function like waves hitting the shore of a beach. The world speaks to you. The fact is, after all, that the world is changing regardless of our wordily intentions. Words can bring us closer to or illuminate parts of the world, but just like no author will ever be able to write a one-to-one biography, there simply is more to life than what we can grasp by putting letters together into words and words into sentences. Mindfulness as presymbolic means that you don't decide to speak but rather let go of yourself—that is, your own agenda—in order to be spoken. This is a bit like how a sound or a smell can make your head turn without you consciously deciding to optimize your hearing by turning around. Being presymbolic may give mindfulness an exotic tinge, as well as hindering a third-person evaluation. The point is that you don't practice mindfulness to experience something specific but to eventually reach peace of mind or equanimity. You are encouraged to be mindful of all sensations, including those that you can't describe. For this reason, many teachers also use poetry to merge better with what happens.

Meditation can be seen as taking refuge in "how," not "why," something happens. This, I believe, also makes the practice impersonal. It's not you that is interesting but how you may relate; it's the relationship that matters. It resembles writing, where you have to be a traitor; as Deleuze says, "it is to create. One has to lose one's identity, one's face, in it. One has to disappear, to become unknown . . . the aim of writing is to carry life to the state of a non-personal power."[110]

Accordingly, mirror thought doesn't refer to a kind of representation of something already given, as in taken for granted. On the contrary, the mind reflects what is presently happening as it is happening and does so in the exact way that it is happening to become with whatever you're doing as a way of actualizing each moment's potential.

The concept "mirror thought" touches on an ontological problem: whether "to be" is to be a "thing" that can be represented. However, because being is presymbolic, we must assume that "to be" doesn't necessarily refer or belong to a certain kind of thing—that is, something can be real without being classifiable. The mirror doesn't lie to me, but that is not the same as it revealing everything; after all, I am more than the phenomenon that I see in the mirror. Goldstein clarifies this when he says, "The moment of opening to the unconditioned, nirvana, confirms most deeply the liberating emptiness of self. In that moment we come to zero. Zero is perhaps the most powerful number: it adds nothing and transforms everything. It is no thing, and yet it is not nothing."[111]

I would not claim that there is nothing, but what is there is virtual—real but not yet actualized. This emphasizes how philosophy is an active practice that produces new values or possibilities of life. Furthermore, some phenomenological philosophers suggest that there is a mirror relationship between thought, language, and the world. Here, thought can be understood from the perspective of the thought itself and not from the agents of power that tell us what to think; instead, ideas and concepts are developed within thought. The images of thought, therefore, emerge from a problem—an invented problem—like the fact that pure forces of being, such as smiling, laughing, loving, and hating, can't really be objectified, only actualized. What does a smile make possible? Even when I smile at my children, my smile doesn't only come because of them—that is to say, due to our closeness or intimacy. There is also something else in between; perhaps this is why the people we know the most, the ones we care most about, also seem to be the biggest strangers in our lives.

They affect us in unpredictable ways.

Another obvious problem is the aforementioned problem of being present. The breathing, for example, is anchored in the present moment. We might think that we are presently aware, but, once we think, we are already thinking about something that we do not perceive. We step outside the flux of life. The problem with being present is that even the present moment is fluctuating; it is not a thing or an object we can study. Being present addresses the fundamental question of existence: Do we follow a metaphysic of becoming or one of being? To frame this differently, does the meditator observe from an unchangeable position, or is he or she also becoming someone else?

"Coming to zero brings us beyond the something-ness of self."[112]

This leads us to the next definition of mindfulness: a nonjudgmental observation. You should not reject anything in advance of experiencing it, just as you should not expect anything. I agree. Nonjudgmental touches upon the idea that the practice is presymbolic since it is without a meta-language. There is no lucrative or untouchable position from which we can evaluate life; everything is a part of life. Furthermore, nonjudgmental touches upon the view of philosophy as the formulation of problems, and as the mismatch of thoughts and perception. Sometimes, we cannot see, feel, or even know what makes us smile. Yet, this nonjudgmental observation is also something that distinguishes mindfulness from Buddhism. Some suggest that "nonjudgmentally" is an invention of Kabat-Zinn.[113]

Nonjudgmental awareness, however, does not mean that we become ignorant, like someone crossing the street on a red light, but rather that we cannot know in advance. For example, we cannot know beforehand how we should live our lives or how we should engage with the world. After all, we become critically aware through a joint companionship between our minds, our bodies, and the world we are placed in. Critique is part of an active form of life, where life matters.

In Buddhism, on the other hand, you can know beforehand because the Buddha already walked a path that led to nirvana. Philosophy, as presented here, is not about following a path but is about inventing paths. Not judging beforehand is a way of cultivating our acceptance that there is no reason to cling or attach to anything specific. The nonjudgmental approach, therefore, is closer to an ongoing and instantaneous evaluation occurring without a guidebook in our hands. Nonjudgmental stresses that the evaluation takes places in the present, living moment, which again requires awareness of what is internal and external. The body, says Colebrook, "is a relation to what is not itself, a movement or an activity from a point of difference to other point of difference."[114] The body is related to becoming in that you are responsible for your own body, as well as what you pass on (i.e., affirm). The latter is where I detect a difference between mindfulness and Deleuze. However, some meditators would describe this difference as one between new-age meditation and serious meditation; for example, Pablo d'Ors writes: "I meditate to make my life meditation; I live to make my meditation life. I don't breathe to contemplate, rather being contemplative is much like being without short of breath."[115]

Mindfulness is a nonconceptual awareness. The experience is direct, without any filter or medium. Mindfulness is not thinking *about,* but being aware of the experience that one is "thinking about." Similarly, philosophy is not the art of contemplating or reflecting *about.* "Contemplations, reflections and communication are not disciplines but machines for constituting Universals in every discipline."[116] Philosophy is, instead, a discipline that involves the creation of concepts. Such creation is always extraordinary or remarkable. "If one concept is 'better' than an earlier one, it is because it makes us aware of new variations and unknown resonances . . . it brings forth an Event that surveys us."[117] So, here the concept sharpens our senses, and philosophy is an ongoing process of seeing more and better. The point is that you will know nothing through concepts unless you have created them in relation to the "Event," in which nothing happens but everything changes. The concept has a history, but it also has becoming—it vibrates between the past and the present. The event is interesting when applied to a concept like "nonjudgmental." It makes sense to stress the importance of a nonjudgmental approach due to the higher level of moralizing, idealizing, and social pressure regarding social status and prestige in today's achievement obsessed society. It can be difficult to find the courage to critically resist this social pressure, as well as to be creative and courageous enough to explore and create your own path.

Thus, because we are formed by what is not us, we also become responsible for what is not us (cf. "write for this people who are missing"). Such responsibility touches upon a delicate spot in mindfulness, mostly in its more new-age iterations, as some teachers favor not only a healthy self-compassion but also a problematic self-love as the prerogative for being able to relate to others. Self-love, as I have already mentioned, is just pure egoism.

In *The Unbearable Lightness of Being*, Milan Kundera ponders the word *compassion*: "In language that derives from Latin, 'compassion' means: we cannot look on coolly as others suffer; or, we sympathize with those who suffer. Another word with approximately the same meaning, 'pity', . . . connotes certain condescension towards the sufferer. 'To take pity on a woman' means that we are better off than she, that we stoop to her level, lower ourselves." According to Kundera, compassion may inspire suspicion, if it operates with an ideal, for example, a superior position from which I judge: "It must be sad to live like that!." "To love someone out of compassion means not really to love," as Kundera says. This emphasizes that self-compassion is not self-love, as mentioned earlier. The etymological roots of compassion can esteem from either "suffering" or from "feeling" so that compassion becomes "co-feeling" (Kundera); you feel with another person's joy, anxiety, or pain, including your own. Similarly, self-compassion in mindfulness consists of two important elements: first is that the outside always constitutes being, and we are all interdependent and changeable; second, in continuation, compassion is more related to altruistic love. Of course, some may claim that if I care for what is not me, because I am constituted by what is not me, then this is actually egoism. Therefore, I suggest something like this: I care for what is not me because I care for life. This emphasizes that I don't own anything—not even my own life. Life is something that passes through me, which emphasizes that I can't control what happens to me yet still learn to respond wisely.

In continuation hereof, mindfulness is nonegoistic alertness, meaning that a mindful person is not referring his or her experiences to his or her own self. Even if you experience strong feelings, you're encouraged to acknowledge these as a present-moment experience. However, you shouldn't identify with them. Feelings are seen as merely visitors in your life. Mindfulness is awareness of change. There can be something healing in just accepting that things are changing: birth, growth, maturity, and death. To meditate is to let go, and letting go is to accept. Furthermore, a nonegoistic alertness is, I suggest, also mandatory for empathy since empathy is not relating the other person's experiences to your own but literally to become with that person's sufferings or joys.

Lastly, mindfulness is participatory observation that expresses, among other things, that the self is constantly being constructed or formed; it's a process of self-transformation. To put it differently: There is no permanent self, no egoistic alertness, because "I" am being constantly formed or affected by what happens. The self is a process—that is, a constant becoming other. While "I" participate, "I" also observe how "I" turns into something else—another.

Thus, since the self is a process, and since everything

is changing (i.e., physically, emotionally, and mentally), mindfulness is an investigation. Being mindful means paying attention to that moment-to-moment reality. The purpose of meditation practice is to pay attention even at trivial times—that is, to be presently aware. This corresponds with how philosophy is questioning what we take for granted—the obvious.

* * * *

"Simplicity is the whole secret of well-being," wrote Peter Matthiessen in his classic travel book, *The Snow Leopard*. I believe he is right. However, based on these definitions in so-called plain English, I wonder whether mindfulness is that simple. Still, the definitions stress certain challenges in order to propose a philosophy of mindfulness. For example, philosophy deals with how a life is formed and forms life as such. Or, put more simply: the philosopher (like the artist) composes alternative worlds that constitute new forms of life. Thus, if the world is on fire, the philosopher aims to create a world in which fire is less likely to flourish. A mindfulness meditator would, on the other hand, try to put out his or her fire—that is, try to overcome capitalism by overcoming his or her own greed. This is not necessarily an either/or situation. I think both are needed. That is, a Bartleby-like approach—"I'd rather not"—but also building something from where future generations can be creative and inventive. The outward approach aims at creating alternatives for the "people who are missing," such as those with fewer privileges, those who suffer from discrimination and violence, etc.

16

MINDFULNESS FACILITATES A RATHER BASIC HUMAN CA-
pacity—for example, waking up and realizing how "survival of the fittest" actually brings an end to lives; instead,
life only remains alive if someone cares for it. It is care that
makes life productive.

Kabat-Zinn's book *Full Catastrophe Living* describes mindfulness as an engagement with life to live a
more healthy and integrated life. However, it is an engagement that is not performance oriented, although regu-
lar practice is needed. The stoic philosophers spoke about
how healthy it can be not to get involved. Mindfulness is
closely related to Western philosophy, where you can get
to know yourself better by taking care of yourself. Deceiving ourselves is generally considered unhealthy, mainly because it is healthier to live honestly than just being
polite. Even the famous pessimist Arthur Schopenhauer
mentions "health" as the most important factor regarding
human happiness, which, of course, refers to a healthy

mind and body. "My body and my will are one," he said.[118] Similarly, the Greek philosophers Plato and Aristotle both saw a healthy body and mind as two inseparable pillars of human existence to nurture more disciplined and ethical coherent citizens. The joy of life finds its expression in Greek philosophy through various plays, whether in sports, dance, or theater. As the saying goes, "*mens sana in corpore sano*", which is Latin for "a healthy mind in a healthy body." This relationship also affects your nutrition; for example, people who are suffering from stress often eat more junk food and do fewer physical activities. In short, they are not paying attention to how they are living their lives. They are just trying to move on, creating a fortress around their own fictional self and the world.

A healthy body is not the same as a beautiful body, if by beauty we refer to the unhealthy desire in contemporary society to look forever young and unwrinkled. Socrates is depicted as small and choppy; yet, he also appears to be rather healthy. For example, he walks a lot in Athens, and he gets up early in the morning, even after enjoying a symposium full of alcoholic liquor.

The subtitle of *Full Catastrophe Living* is "How to cope with stress, pain and illness using mindfulness meditation." Such a title refers to the first noble truth, but it also addresses a sick contemporary society. One may ask whether mindfulness is used as a bandage that works like a numbing spray on a bruise during a football game so that the player can go on playing the same game, or whether they want to change the game—that is, society. For many, unfortunately, mindfulness is just used as a Band-Aid solution; however, if you really live mindfully, then you will interact with society differently. This is my, perhaps naïve, postulate. Saying it differently: there are certain things you can't witness without changing how you live, act, and think. What counts, of course, are your acts more than your words. With wisdom comes silence. For obvious reasons, it is not communication that we lack today, but places for reflection and silence. Similarly, you should be skeptical when business organizations become mindful or claim to lead according to Aristotle or Plato, especially if they basically still act the same. Then the problem is not related to Plato or mindfulness but to the fact that some people only speak about saving the planet, yet they don't really try to act accordingly. There is a lot of feel-good spirituality and symbolism in the world, perhaps because it is good business. This doesn't mean that mindfulness can't contribute to all aspects of life, including business, but rather that there is a real difference between doing business mindfully or not. There are certain forms of actions that you can only continue doing if you're not being very mindful.

Nevertheless, when you're stressed, it is difficult to live in the moment and be efficient, and it is also difficult to be caring and compassionate. There is a difference between reacting or responding to the stimuli that constantly reach us and affect us. When we react, we are typically slaves to our feelings; we tend to become impulsive and rely on our default setting, with the result that we rarely make adequate decisions. For a simple example, we eat sugar or drink alcohol when a nap would be more appropriate. However, if you pay attention and become aware of what is happening, then it is often easier to add perspectives and understand what needs to be done. The challenge is to invent a problem, not look for already available solutions, because this would hinder your interaction with what happens.

For example, mindfulness may help regulate your approach to life, to cultivate a more balanced and harmonious lifestyle, and to notice significant changes in your behavior. Likewise, Aristotle spoke about building excellence in character, which is when you act appropriately to the situation and want to act so. The idea is that you can train your attention to both differentiate between the many problems that a situation may confront you with and understand your feelings better in order to give a more fruitful response to what is happening. If you're aware, you will also notice how you're affected before you react. Therefore, in real-life situations, mindfulness appears as an intervening time, although in reality, you're aware of what happens while it happens. "The decision rests on with perception," says Aristotle.[119] You need to be present and consciously aware in a particular situation in order to evaluate. In other words, there is no general principle that can decide for us beforehand; there is no higher set of values or norms. Rather, as Aristotle mentions, you need to be on the spot to decide whether the bread is properly cooked or not.

17

ONE OF THE MOST CITED DEFINITIONS OF MINDFULNESS comes from Kabat-Zinn: "Mindfulness means paying attention in a particular way: on purpose, in the present moment, and non-judgmentally."[120] The definition consists of four elements, where the first seems to be the most important, but since it refers to something particular, the four elements operate on an equal level:

1. Paying attention *in a particular way*
2. On purpose
3. In the present moment
4. Non-judgmentally

"Pay attention" is both a request and an invitation. "On purpose" signifies that we need to establish some effort or motivation to accept this invitation, especially since what we should pay attention to is life as such, not just something that we already find pleasurable because such "pleasure" only cements that we have a problem with craving or attachment. Furthermore, doing something on purpose requires that one knows something *about* a certain thing. Therefore, I believe that cultivating this purpose of paying attention emphasizes that a mindful person does something on purpose, not that he or she is aware of something specific on purpose. Furthermore, "on purpose" is an acknowledgement of the story that the Buddha shared; due to your belief in this story, you wish to participate in this practice. Testing it, reviewing it, and revising it are all things that the many commentators are doing—transforming one's self, etc.

Mindfulness is not a determination; it does not refer to any particular object. All directions are equal. For example, one can't point to the present moment because it constantly changes. Just like reading the same book over and over, where each reading is different from the previous due to the flow of time. In that sense, you can't do the same thing twice; you can only repeat your approach.

Mindfulness is a practice of non-doing—that is, not doing anything to achieve another goal apart from being mindful. For example, a mindful person directs his or her mind towards whatever is happening, and he or she directs his or her awareness to the present moment in order to observe. Be with whatever is in the midst of becoming.

About the adjective *quodlibet* (i.e., whatever), Italian philosopher Giorgio Agamben says that it is often translated, as "it does not matter which, indifferently"; however, he also emphasizes that in its etymological form, the Latin says exactly the opposite: "being such that it always matters." *Being such that it always matters* could serve as a beautiful definition of a mindful philosophy placed in between the particular and the general.[121]

* * * *

Mindfulness is a radical openness, a kind of exposure. Thus, it is on purpose that we are aware. Awareness matters. The tricky part, of course, is why we should pay attention to our perceptions more than the memories that they might awaken. The point is, though, that our memory changes as well. As we expose ourselves, our "self" or "I" also transforms. "I will never again know what I am, where I am, from where I'm from, where I'm going, through where to pass. I am exposed to others, to foreign things."[122]

I suggest that the idea of "my" story as a coherent narrative crumbles away and gives room for episodic stories that examine how I am becoming another. It made sense when the French poet Arthur Rimbaud said, "*Je est un autre,*" meaning "I is someone else." He deliberately disobeyed the rules of grammar, mixing first-person singular with third-person singular. Later, Rimbaud wrote, "Right now, I'm beshitting myself as much as possible. Why? I want to be a poet, and I'm working to turn myself into a *seer* . . . It has to do with making your way towards the unknown by a derangement of *all the sense* . . . It's wrong to say *I think*: one should say *I am thought*."[123]

What Rimbaud pointed out is that you can only transform if you let go of your illusions—the illusion of being in control or the illusion of seeing yourself as a fixed and unchangeable "self." Rimbaud makes fun of the "many *egoists*" that call themselves authors.

The main thread in your life is often described as being red, like a bloodline, but I propose it is red because your life is on fire; the reasonable thread is gone, burned (or burn it to liberate yourself). Often all these narratives turn into a pretext for doing nothing but making well-argued excuses: "My father made me do it," "I am the reincarnation of . . . ," "It goes back to my mum; she, too, was . . ."

Rimbaud said that it is okay to be disturbed or confused; in fact, he encouraged the acceptance of disorder or chaos as a state of being that forces one's creativity and inventions. He knew that becoming a poet was courageous and generous, as it meant seeing new possible relations. It was, in his words, to be *thought*.

Getting to experience Rimbaud's words requires more than a few hours of practice for most people. For this reason, most mindfulness programs run for six to eight weeks, which may confront participators with the strength of their intentions because the time frame illustrates how willing they are to put in the work to become more mindful. It does not come for free. Perhaps the time frame can be seen as a tentative guide to whether an introduction to mindfulness is legit or part of the business world's need for a quick two-day seminar-fixing approach. Since the consensus in today's achievement society is that time is money, it may explain why people perform or sell some mindfulness programs with little experience and for a short period of time. The convincing argument lies in the practice—that is, the experience. You pay attention to the present moment on purpose, which means that you actually do not direct your attention or awareness toward anything specific but to the flow of time passing. That is, how one now turns into the past as a new now emerges; time is a successive change. It's living unfolding. Experimenting with the present living moment to moment.

What the participants are doing is "non-doing." Non-doing is not synonymous with doing nothing because consciousness and intention (i.e., purpose) matter. "Non-doing simply means letting things be and allowing them to unfold in their own way . . . Meditation is synonymous with the practice of non-doing. We aren't practicing, to make things perfect or to do things perfectly. Rather, we practice to grasp and realize (make real for ourselves) the fact that things already are perfect, perfectly what they are."[124] So, non-doing is entering a state of contemplation or allowing things to slow down before you act. Therefore, meditation alone will rarely change the world but will often lead to a more cautious way of acting and contributing to life. For this reason, mindfulness can be seen as a fruitful uprising against short-term thinking that characterizes contemporary society. It's a way of cultivating more sustainable approaches to life.

This resembles how Gandhi's nonviolence was the act of being nonviolent. Non-doing, of course, contrasts the urge of contemporary society to perform, to measure, and to compare. Once again, this also touches on the problem of judgment or nonjudgment. Instead of striving toward a certain idea, your relationship with life is a dynamic tightrope walk. As you consciously experience what takes place—the thoughts and feelings that pass—you gradually connect in more beneficial ways. The wisdom functions like the world: it is integrated with the world; all it requires is awareness. Thus, the participants who are practicing mindfulness "are actively turning in to each moment in an effort to remain awake and aware from one moment to the next. They practice mindfulness."[125] What I emphasize when trying to outline a philosophy of mindfulness is that it is not only you turning inwards but also outwards, because what you experience is life; it is life that makes you alive.

What is good or bad depends on how you live your life. No one knows what to destroy, protect, or create (i.e., cultivate) before he or she begins noticing what actually happens. "In Nature there is neither Good or Evil . . . If men were born free, they would form no concept of good and evil so long as they remained free,"[126] Deleuze says, referring to Spinoza. Instead, there are good and bad things for each mode of existence—that is, depending on how we relate to what happens. This is why experiencing plays such a crucial role in mindfulness, not the simplicity of the theory.

What does it open up for? How does it work? Is it beneficial?

* * * *

Let's return to the notion "on purpose." The point is that—if we recall that the word *sati* comes from the verb "to remember"—when I see my son smile, his smile is the object of my seeing. If I then remember the smile, I think *about* that past event, and then the smile is an object of my memory. Although mindfulness stresses the first—because the latter is a memory of my son's smile—the practice implicitly plays on one's past experiences . . . those brief moments of awareness that everyone has experienced (e.g., moments of flow). Remembering also plays an important role not only in the Buddhist traditions but also in philosophy. For example, Merleau-Ponty says, "But in reality I would not know that I possess a true idea if my memory did not enable me to relate what is now evident with what was evident a moment ago."[127] Memory refers, then, both to my memory as well as to the collective. Once again, this touches on how our perception and memory affect one another and, at times, can make us less narrow-minded as when those with the power portray the past in a certain light. It also stresses how remembering moments of pure awareness in our past can motivate us to concentrate in the actual present moment. The moral is that we do not want to miss our life. In other words, when I see my son's smile, I must see his eyes, and not be thinking about the past or the present. Each present moment is already gone as I am thinking about it. Then, once he turns around the corner, I can recall the smile to comfort myself, but I should not dwell on the smile because then I would just miss being present in the next moment and so forth. So, why should I pay attention and not just let my mind wander when I can't really recall this moment? First of all, I can if I want to, but the reason why I should pay attention is to be aware in the moment and secure a good storage of my experiences so that I can use these once I recognize that his smile has changed. I can learn from my past experiences without reliving them over and over. However, awareness also means seeing things as they are, which is that my son's smile is actually impermanent. Therefore, awareness in each moment is also an investment in not missing out on anything.

To remember comes from the Latin word *recordor,* which includes the Latin word for heart *cor*. It signifies that our memories pass through our heart; they affect us, form us. The heart may just be a muscle, but as a metaphor, we all know what it means to keep certain memories in our hearts. Do our memories restrain or liberate us? Hearts, however, need to be nurtured as well because we have been seduced into treasuring something that in reality was unhealthy. History has shown us how dictators, political turbulence, or financial misery can seduce or manipulate people into believing that war, discrimination, and even hate are acceptable. Still, we treasure our memories close to our hearts. The idea of being mindful "on purpose," therefore, is also a reminder that we are alive . . . to enjoy the simple joy of being here and not already long gone perhaps and capable of leaving a memory in some other people's lives . . . a heartfelt gratitude to our previous formation and our present level of maturity; this sounds like a philosophy's love of wisdom. This also illustrates that the philosopher is not the one who is sage but is the one who is compliant to wisdom.

The freedom to live and experience is not in textbooks but is performed through how we actualize this thing called life. The freedom lies in our intention to live our lives fully. Rimbaud opens *Une Saison en Enfer* by writing, "Long ago, if my memory serves, life was a feast where every heart was open, where every wine flowed."[128]

Life is a feast if we have an open, curious, and non-normative approach. If you are around children, you will often notice that they are happy and full of joy. The reason for this, I think, is that they are much more direct in their experiences. They are alive, while we tend to forget that simple fact with age so that our lives become less joyous and more filled with preoccupations, worries, and desires. Children are becoming themselves more naturally than adults. *Becoming* yourself means constantly being born within yourself. I don't intend to refer to a true essence or a kind of self-originating instance; instead, each moment, each minute, each hour, and each day, we wear out our past self, fertilizing our future self. The point is that we were already alive in life. There is nothing else than this. Becoming is an acceptance that all things are interdependent and coevolving. Furthermore, when there is a non-self, then each one of us is neither inherently good nor bad; we may live better or worse forms of life due to how we relate to our circumstances. This relationship with life becomes, I believe, even more important today when the dominant mind-set seems to be capitalism, with its greed and selfishness, but no matter how much people earn, how much prestige and status they can ascribe due to titles and power, they, too, end up becoming who they become. To become one with money or with the nature of life, it's not a question, because there is an unmatchable feast related to being alive. Awareness is a direct emotional experience rather than religious and transcendent understanding; awareness begins with the engagement of the senses. To see, hear, taste, feel, and smell are things we do. We sense with our bodies and minds. I bend down on purpose to really see the scratch on my son's knee, I turn my head to hear what my daughter is screaming about, I touch her forehead to detect any fever, and so on. To cultivate our awareness, we have to pay attention on purpose . .

. the purpose of feeling more alive, more touched, or more intermingled with life as such.

* * * *

Although mindfulness may initially seem to be a rather simple thing, it can actually be quite difficult to practice—that is, practicing nonjudgmental awareness in body, feelings, mind, and dharma. Awareness brings us in attunement with life. But do all forms of life count as equals? How does one pay attention to the present moment on purpose without any kind of judgment? To do something "on purpose" means that there is a reason behind it that makes it less reasonable to pay attention to something else. The argument here is related to time. The claim is that only this moment exists. We may miss out on life. Yet, as already mentioned, the present moment is all there is, even though it doesn't really exist. It's a constant process of actualization that depends on awareness; therefore, I propose understanding "the present moment" and "nonjudgmentally" as strictly operational concepts. Both basically claim the same thing: Don't get caught up in the past; don't worry about the past and what you didn't do, and don't get caught in future planning and fantasies, ideals, and norms that you have to live up to. Don't postpone your life until after you have received or achieved something. Stay in the flux of the moment. See what it has to offer. Still, mindfulness is more than the dogma of "the present moment", dogs are present, but not very mindful. Next to living in the moment, mindfulness is also being aware of our mind, body, and feelings in each present moment. This means that your awareness is stretched out in between your past and future. As a simple example, you are aware of certain feelings, but due to your memory, you know how to act to avoid unbeneficial or unwholesome actions. The question, therefore, is "How is the mind aware of itself without stepping outside the present moment?" This question is not easily answered but is nevertheless part of most mindfulness definitions. Similarly, one monk defines mindfulness as "keeping one's consciousness alive to the present reality."[129] Awareness is a direct experience. It's coupled with compassion or care. It requires ongoing fine-tuning.

* * * *

Awareness may be seen as a lighter form of attention. For example, you may be aware of stimuli without them being at the center of attention. You may be aware of the children screaming outside your window without really paying attention to them. Attention, on the other hand, is a process of focusing or tightening our conscious awareness, which typically means that we narrow our range of experience. That is, when you're with your children, you're with your children, not your phone, etc. When you wash dishes, drink a beer or whatever; you do only those activities. Mindfulness is placed in-between our limited range of experiences that are constantly trying to nurture a more open and receptive range. This is also related to time. Each present moment goes infinitely into both the past and the future. "It [time] flows from today to tomorrow. It flows from today to yesterday; it flows from yesterday to today, from today to today, from tomorrow to tomorrow. It is as if you were sweeping your gaze over one continuous fabric of time. Past time and present time do not accumulate, and future time does not deplete."[130] Thus, the challenge is to be open to the infinite time that each moment carries. To put it differently, you should be cautious not to turn "be here now" or "the present moment" into an ideal. For example, "to wake up" is something that happens in time just as you wake up from a dream; it's a process. What matters is our involvement "now here." How we intervene—what we pass on—is what matters.

Each "present moment" is more like a place where time folds around itself, and it's exactly there that you can make decisions that are liberating. Therefore, the two concepts "in the present moment" and "nonjudgmentally" are ways of helping the practitioner. The simple reason for this is that to be fully aware and attentive in each present living moment is difficult. Once we try to stay with our breathing, we experience this, but we should not blame ourselves (i.e., judging). Only accept that our mind drifts and then guide it gently back to the present moment and our breathing. The key idea is that the only thing that really exists is the experience of this present moment, although each moment is virtual, stretched out in between a past and a future, all waiting to be actualized.

* * * *

In mindfulness, you often learn to meditate by paying attention to your breathing. The breath becomes an anchor that the meditator can return to when his or her mind drifts. When we become aware of how we breathe in and breathe out, then, of course, we are dealing with a limited range of experience. Nevertheless, focusing on the breath helps the mind to pay attention. The limited range of experience doesn't tell us anything about how easy or difficult it is to stay mindful with your breathing. The general consensus among practitioners is that this is far more difficult than it seems mainly because our minds tend to wander. The mind moves from attention toward a default setting of general vague awareness, perhaps even rapid and changing distractions, and it often moves back and forward in time instead of staying in the present moment.

The moral is that the lived experience is more important than knowledge *about*. The preposition "about" indicates a separation, as if I can evaluate my life from above or outside my life. Of course, in practice, we try to place ourselves in a pit stop to get a better view of what is happening, but then we are rationalizing, which, by definition, takes place after what we rationalize about happened. This is not to undermine the need for room for reflection, which I think is important in all aspects of life, but rather to emphasize that there is a difference between living and being parked in a pit stop. It can be tempting for some to prepare to live a specific kind of life that they will never really live, just as too much time learning from our past experiences, reflecting, and rationalizing can hinder us from being moved by what takes place here and now. Although we need to jump back and forth in time, for example, to reflect and learn from mistakes, we should be cautious not to get stuck in this time machine. The point is that the more in contact with life we are, the more qualified we will act regarding the need for reflection. Basically, we know when it is time to take a time-out.

The guiding question is which experience is real?

Portuguese writer Fernando Pessoa illustrates that the concept "present" itself is one that we can too easily become attached to. Pessoa writes:

> Live, you say, in the present
> Live only in the present
> But I don't want the present. I want reality;
>
> . . .
>
> I only want reality, things without time present

For the philosopher, knowledge and wisdom merge with how you're living your life. You live it—life, that is. Philosophy, for example, is not wisdom but a love of wisdom that emphasizes that the philosopher's approach to life is formed by wisdom. He or she is careful with claiming, "This is the truth." This is also why Deleuze often plays on the philosopher being a non-philosopher and vice versa. The philosopher is the person who knows that he or she is no sage; rather, he or she is the nomad being moved by the movement of the earth. Or to put it differently, Pessoa can't hide behind a self or an identity because that would separate him from life. Nor can he live in the present if the present moment is encapsulated and distinct from the flow of reality—that is, what is in the midst of becoming. Instead, he must stay in the open. Paying attention correlates with presence—that is, being involved.

Being involved knows when to accept—that is, let go. It may be useful to accept your life conditions after an accident, if you cannot get your legs back. Here, such difficult acceptance confirms that time is irreversible. Still, it would tend resignation to accept how many children and women are treated in the world by referring to religion or cultural difference, although these just try to cover up repression. In this situation, not doing anything would be unacceptable because we then pass on current problems of repression to future generations. As Nietzsche and Deleuze respectively suggested, "Do you desire this once more and innumerable times more?" Or "*whatever you will, will it in such a way that you also will its eternal return.*" The decisions we make can only liberate if they are not guided by vanity or egoism. Becoming is an impersonal and collective process.

18

MINDFULNESS SHARES THE THREE MARKS OR QUALITIES that define Buddhism: impermanence, suffering, and non-self. All three rank equally, at least in theory (something else in practice.) Based on my experience with different mindfulness teachers, the non-self is often not mentioned. The problem is that the concept "self" has a short but strong history in the West due to the history of psychology that often views the self as a fixed or static entity to which you can live more or less authentically, or a self that can be developed and formed more or less as you wish. Although the latter is closer to the impermanent self of Buddhism, and far more flexible, it still asserts a kind of ownership of the self or "I." For example, "I am in pain" or "I am stressed." Here, "pain" and "stressed" function as objects merged with your body.

In contrast, mindfulness suggests—when it practices non-self—terms such as "This is pain" or "This is stress" to emphasize how we can easily begin to identify ourselves with the world we inhabit—for example, a world full of stress and pain. Yet, if you accept that everything really does change, including your pain, and you become more aware of what may also be part of the world, you may turn into something else.

An important element of an affirmative philosophy where how you experience, experiment with, and actualize (or become) is crucial for living a life worth living is to understand the self as a changing process. I am always another.

Thus, if mindfulness loosens its tied relationship with Western psychology and the "self", then it can move toward becoming a mindful philosophy. This is, however, one of the biggest obstacles.

* * * *

The myth of Narcissus told by Ovid is the story of a young and beautiful man who is also the most conscious of men, or he appears to be. When he sees his own pretty face mirrored on the lake, he becomes conscious of what he wants, and yet, he is unaware that all he really wants is his own image of himself. How many are in love with their self-image today?

Knowledge is part of the passage of becoming conscious or aware.

Today, as I have illustrated earlier, we live in a world full of Narcissuses, almost intoxicated by their own goodness, justice, beauty, etc. They, too, drown from this overdose of self-love. They neglect to understand that what is good can only be viewed by examining which life is good—a changeable practice, not an unchangeable ideal.

To avoid this temptation of narrative self-love, it is important to acknowledge that consciousness, too, is a passage. Consciousness is not an either/or concept. Rather it's a way of enlarging reality; it makes what has happened more real, even in my own mind, not as a way of explaining but of unfolding and refolding. The narrative self is, therefore, not part of a mindful philosophy in its serious form; rather, the self is episodic or a rapture. The famous red thread going through your life can easily be invented in all colors; perhaps a life is a patchwork. "The process of becoming-nomadic is rather a zigzagging itinerary of successive but not linear steps . . . "[131] Life is not a linear progress.

Imagine that I encounter an animal, then I can become animalized—that is, not by crawling and growling like a dog, but rather to impose a quality where forms become indiscernible. This process, according to Deleuze, is a spiritual will that seeks the elementary forces beyond the organic, it is "a spirituality of the body." [132] I incorporate something "beneath representation, beyond representation." Sensation, therefore, is not the same as perceiving because we perceive through identification: I am like . . . looking for the same, the known, the prestigious, what gives status, whereas sensation is pure difference. It deals with intensity, tension, suspense, and excitement . . . to experience life as movement while it moves. In short, when I really experience being alive, I am making contact with life in a way that takes me beyond myself.

* * * *

The first characteristic is impermanence (Anicca)—that is, everything changes. For this reason, everything is also potentially possible; for example, it is possible to transform one's suffering. This is an element that some mindfulness teachers' link with neuroplasticity, which are changes in our neural pathways and synapses due to changes in the environment or our behaviors, thoughts, and feelings, as well as changes in our bodies, for example, impairment. In other words, the brain is not a static organ; it changes through life due to its plasticity. This, of course, does not tell us what the mind is. The mind is not the brain but to become conscious. To be unconscious is to be mindless, unaware, and perhaps even spiritually lazy. More importantly, impermanence confirms that it is our dominating belief in a metaphysic *of being* that makes us suffer. The problem is that a certain being functions as a stable ideal or norm that encourages, or even forces, people to live up to inhabiting such a being. In other words, it's problematic not to question what is real. Such blind belief in own truths can be seen in religion, political ideologies, and within science as well.

Traditionally, there is a consensus from pre-Socratic philosophers and Buddhist monks to the critical thinking of the Frankfurter School that we human beings *do* too much. Some even suggest that we have turned ourselves into human doers rather than human beings. The point is that we in the Western world live in a performance society in which doing rather than being is the norm. I agree with this critique. Yet, I disagree when it comes to how we should or ought to be, because the only way we actually can be is by becoming something else.

Therefore, the metaphysics of being may serve as a contemporary critique of stress, performance, competition, acceleration, and doing, doing, doing, but it does so, at least most of the time, by changing one ideal with another. It becomes a battlefield between diverging norms. After all, people are stressed because of the norms and ideals related to capitalism—that is, the prestige, status, identity, and power associated with money and positions. Another ideal is to just be true, honest, or authentic; however, this is only possible if we acknowledge that this basically is to become and not live up to a certain ideal. Being is becoming, unless we are already dead. In other words, I urge all to be critically aware when reading philosophy or practicing Buddhism or mindfulness in order to notice whether the approach to experiencing life more richly is reduced to a strategy for experiencing a certain kind of reality. Be cautious if you hear statements such as "That's the way life is" or "This is the real x," looking for universalities where there are none. A too-rigid approach is funnily described by Catherine Lacey in her novel *Nobody Is Ever Missing* (a title that indirectly tells us that there is no fixed self). She writes, *"Seashore, sister, seagull—which does not belong?* But my life, anyone's life, any life like a real life, any life that is humanlike—it can't be turned into questions like that."

A process is defined by never becoming a finished action. A process is a process of actualization. What there actually is, therefore, is constituted by its becoming—a process of becoming never reaches a conclusion. You can't really say, "This is a true woman" without both discriminating against many women but also breaking the process.

For this reason, Nietzsche also spoke about affirming what is different and not just confirming what is known and fits a predefined or desired being; instead, an affirmation of difference opens us to the joy of knowing ourself to be different.

What is the joy of remaining the same throughout life? To find balance in life is a dynamic process. To balance is a verb—a doing word. Knowing oneself is different is a matter of coming into contact with what is real. Experimenting. Exploring. And what is real is that everything changes, including one's self.

The second characteristic is that there is no self or ego. The self is an empty appearance. If we see this claim through the first, it becomes easier to accept. The permanent instant or moment is constantly changing. Each now turns into another now, and another, and another, and so forth in a continuous movement. Of course, you don't change completely from one instant to the next. I can still recognize my children when I pick them up after school, and they can still recognize me. Yet, at times, they surprise me: they are different due to the affections they experienced in school (or I experienced reading and writing while they were at school; something always happens in between). If we look from a distance, then each moment brings us closer to death. It feels like time becomes less and less, although a minute is a minute is a minute. Time is linear, irreversible, and circular. Similarly, you can change your character intentionally, for example, by practicing loving kindness, just as such a change can happen due to drastic changes in your life or surroundings either internally or externally. "Sometimes a man undergoes such changes that I should hardly have said he was the same man . . . what shall we say of infants?"[133] Children often find it strangely funny that their parents were once babies as well because it does not fit with their current picture of their parents.

The third characteristic is that life is suffering, from birth to death because of sickness, loss, unfulfilled desires and wishes, etc. Nature is full of suffering. Destruction and creation go hand in hand just as life and death do. In Buddhist teachings, there are three forms of suffering: 1) the suffering of suffering, 2) the suffering of change, and 3) the suffering of conditioned existence.[134] Each level is related to the three characteristics: impermanence, non-ego/non-self, and suffering.

The suffering of suffering refers to the kind of suffering with which mindfulness operates. For example, you suffer from stress, anxiety, or depression. The second form of suffering is related to impermanence or change—that is, the impermanence of everything; for example, our bodies change, we grow old, our children grow old, they move away, we experience sickness, and we die. The third level of suffering is more fundamental because it refers to the idea that there is no self. Or, as Lopez writes, "that our minds and bodies are so conditioned that we are always subject to suffering in the next moment. This is because our existence depends upon causes and conditions over which we have no control."[135] Becoming mindful is a process that never stops, or it stops when one truly experiences that he or she is dissolved in life as such.

Another way of illustrating this is to emphasize that you only really overcome the suffering of suffering by accepting the two other kinds of suffering. If you focus on only the first step, then it can be far too tempting to remain attached to an idea of a lucrative self. For example, "Now I don't suffer because I am mindful" can easily turn into people who cry over their own capacity to be good or be touched if they experience other people's suffering. There is a difference between believing that you can decide and accepting that life comes onto you. You can change your relationship but just invent new versions of your self. Choosing the balanced choice has nothing to do with the "best practice" or "best fit." Becoming is much more unpredictable.

Author F. Scott Fitzgerald wrote the following illuminating quote: "Perhaps fifty percent of your friends and relations will tell you in good faith that it was my drinking that drove Zelda mad, and the other half would assure you that it was her madness that drove me to drink. Neither of these judgments means much of anything. These two groups of friends and relations would be unanimous in saying that each of us would have been much better off without the other. The irony is that we have never been more in love with each in all of our lives. She loves the alcohol on my lips. I cherish her most extravagant hallucinations. In the end, nothing really had much importance. We destroyed ourselves. But in all honesty, I never thought we destroyed each other."[136]

All normative predictions or habitual assumptions crumble away. Fitzgerald writes from a position that feeds on the difference that matters, which is that the lovers—perhaps rather hopelessly naïve or romantic—try to repeat the intensive feeling of being in love. The kiss being caused by alcohol that is caused by the hallucination that is caused by the kiss that is . . . Lines of life crisscross one another. What matters is that your involvement in life is un-strategic; otherwise, it is not really open. Mindfulness matters when it doesn't present you with a position in opposition to something, as if you could establish a distance to life; rather, it begins in the middle while it is mixed with life.

I have only one preference: to go where life takes me.

ENCOUNTERS

19

A PHILOSOPHY OF MINDFULNESS IS NOT A STEP dance between the mind and the political, the personal and the social. They are intermingled. The experience is not given to me like a fact. Rather, what I experience in the world and how I experience it constitutes me. The world is not out there fixed and done. It doesn't come to me like a wave; rather, I form and am being formed by the world. I am affected by the world just as I affect it.

The intimate relationship between the world and me resembles the relationship between the mind and the body. They are connected. "What is a passion in the mind is *also* a passion in the body, what is an action in the mind is *also* an action in the body. Parallelism thus excludes any eminence of the soul, any spiritual and moral finality, any transcendence of a God who might base one series on the other."[137] A human being becomes a part of the world, and the world becomes a part of him or her. There is a dynamic relationship. "Emotions are not objects, things that we own. They emerge from an encounter between oursel-ves-and-the-world . . . We are emotions and relationships. We cannot stand outside ourselves."[138]

We are the way we—our bodies and minds—relate to the world. Your approach to life is your philosophy. If your approach is open, aware, humble, and caring, you will gradually transform because no ideals or hidden agendas are hindering your movements.

Gradually, we will explore what we—our bodies and minds—are capable of doing. According to Spinoza, all a body can do (in a nonviolent manner) is also its right. It is the body's right to terminate relations that poison it and establish relations that make it stronger. Hereby, we don't say what a body should eat or not eat, for example, only that there is a clear difference between poison and food. Also, a body is in its right to establish other relations that better fit its nature. It emphasizes the will to do what we can, not just do what we will. If you can organize your life differently—for example, spending less time acting as a professional, which may drain you or leave you sad—then it is in your right to change such relations. Being connected with life is similar to being energized.

Spinoza refers to the concept *conatus*, which is Latin for striving and energy. It is something that all bodies possess both internally and externally; it preserves its existence (i.e., energy), but it also strives to grow . . . to experience being alive. It uses energy to live, but living also gives energy, for example, when we touch one another or are touched by nature or art. *Conatus*, therefore, is a mode of existence or life-form that "comes to exist when its extensive parts are extrinsically determined to enter into the relation that characterizes the mode: then, and only then, is its essence itself determined as *conatus*."[139]

It affirms the notion that that which brings life correlates with how a body can function. For this reason, *conatus* is related to power or strength (i.e., the capacity for being affected as a maximum position and a minimum position) and the variations of power of acting or the forces of existing within these positive limits. Living a life worth living relates to our desire to be touched by life.

Thus, your level of energy and striving to remain alive depends on what you encounter. How does what happens affect me? What thoughts and feelings arise in me? These questions illustrate how we become conscious. "The *conatus* having become conscious of itself under this or that affect is called desire, desire always being a desire for something."[140] Desire here is not guided by a lacking; on the contrary, it is a process of joy where everything is permitted but not everything is followed. We should follow life—not ideals, norms, or laws. This process is non-dual because what affects you also affects *conatus*. The challenge—an ethical challenge—is to distinguish what determines or forms us from that which we determine or form. It's a process of becoming worthy of what happens in the sense that you can match it. Acceptance, however, is not resignation. Non-doing is a powerful form of action.

What your body and mind can do is also their right. For example, it is also in your right to say no. It is your right to refuse to set objectives. It is your right to refuse being happy all the time. It is your right to be angry or sad for a while. That men and women are not treated as equal, in all aspects of life, makes me angry. It makes me sad when I see terror and violence in the world. And as an angry man, I don't want to fight with my fist; instead, I propose that, among other things, we acknowledge how a metaphysic of being is an unhealthy starting point for any humanistic research program. For this reason, the so-called happiness industry often produces more anxiety and stress than actual moments of happiness, mainly because it presents an idea where it appears as if it is not okay to be unhappy—that is, being happy turns into a norm. So, let me make it clear: it can be rather healthy to dwell on the past and be angry and skeptical toward the future. The point is not to remain angry, sad, or full of fear all the time, which seems quite obvious, but similar to being happy all the time, appears as living a life within an impenetrable shell. For example, the opposite of joy is not sadness but anger. You can verify this by being with children. If you stop their playing, which often is full of joy, then they don't move to sadness but find it annoying to stop something they like. To like and not like are based on their experiences, now and here—not moral ideals about good and bad.

The argument for not anticipating the present living moment with predefined ideals and norms is that we don't really know what this moment asks of us, just as we don't know what we are capable of. Ethics become a compositional power because the stronger the affection—for example, accepting "There is anger in me"—the greater our capacity to act. Accepting is part of a nonjudgmental approach. Don't judge yourself for experiencing this emotion, but explore the situation.

It's a way of balancing reason with emotions, mind with body.

How can you find a decent balance between what is good for you (i.e., strive) and the arousal that you experience (i.e., level of energy)? The question is not that simple because most people have experienced being aroused by something that was not good for them, either because it involved poisoning their bodies and minds or because they passed on unhealthy seeds to a fellow living being with whom they share the planet. For a similar reason, mindfulness is not about following your heart but cultivating it—cultivating it according to your own experiences but also the experiences that are generated in the social community that we all are a part of. You are always placed in interplay with other people, other forms of organization that you may try to reorganize, but always with a respect for how it is now. Cultivation happens with care and compassion, not threats or physical force.

The balance between your body and mind is to acknowledge how the body often outsmarts the mind. It leaves us with the question of whether we are being unconsciously seduced or whether the heart needs to be cultivated to be more than a muscle that pumps blood through a net of arteries and veins. Placed somewhere in between, conatus attempts to preserve that which is good for us. Similar to Buddhism, conatus always involves the power to act. "Enlightenment does not happen because we have gotten rid of a certain amount of karmic activity. It happens when our mind cuts through delusion . . . It depends on the quality of our awareness, of balance and wisdom in the moment."[141] Like anywhere else, you also learn from your mistakes in Buddhism. Mistakes are experiences that make us wiser and, therefore, able to make more mature decisions. So, yes, the present moment is all there is, but this is connected with an infinite past and future. Everything changes, even what actually made yesterday a good experience for us.

Spinoza says that "we neither strive for, nor will, neither want, nor desire anything because we judge it to be good; on the contrary, we judge something to be good because we strive for it, will it, want it, and desire it."[142]

The good that Spinoza mentions does not refer to an abstract or transcendent category—for instance, a Platonic idea that, per definition, should be reasonable and justifiable to desire. On the contrary, the good comes from within as a hunger or appetite for living. Such an appetite develops due to your life experiences. Mindfulness can help to distinguish unhealthy desires from what is typically called more "skillful motivation." The latter basically refers to nurturing better contact with life. Knowing what needs to be done and what limits need to be set for us to accomplish what we desire is skillful. However, we should not see desire as a narrow ego trip; on the contrary, the desire of Spinoza is to cultivate a capacity to become with life as such.

Literature is a way of empathy where both the writer and the reader extend their ability to be another person, another living being (e.g., an animal) or a nonorganic being (e.g., a robot) to feel, think, and experience the trademarks of this character's sensibility. All art aims at knowing something other than yourself.

Thus, my call for a philosophy of mindfulness is also an argument for placing greater importance on the humanities – including literature and other arts. Art presents us with a neutral method that aims at drawing various images of the human being, whether that person lives in the labyrinths of Istanbul as in Orhan Pamuk's novels, or whether Tracey Emin invites us in to her bed, where the bedsheets are covered with bodily secretions (*My Bed*, 1999). Art can help us broaden our mind and mature our spirit. It's not just as if being mindful is good and mindless is bad; rather that paying attention can make us aware of what is a better way for us to act. We can problematize the causes, evaluate our actions, and improve our decisions. For example, Emin's unmade bed with visible stained bedsheets challenges our ideas about how a bed *should* look; hereby the piece shows how its contribution is relevant. Art questions how we justify our beliefs, for example, regarding our fictional idea about women's clean beds; it contests our beliefs and widens our understanding of the world we live in. Instead of being mainly an intellectual exercise experiencing art affects our perception, it impregnates us bodily and emotionally. And it's experiences like these that may make us more humble toward the greatness and diversity of life.

* * * *

To live fully is to experience a balance between the body, feelings, and mind. In other words, it does not make sense to strive for something if your body and mind are not in agreement. Some may argue that it is reasonable that you should work extra hours to gain more profit, but if working more hours affects your body negatively due to the intensity and pressure, then, of course, it is not reasonable. Similarly, your feelings can interfere or contradict your mental judgment. The main point is only to strive, will, and want what corresponds with our bodily needs. If not, then you are seduced or manipulated to neglect your bodily desires, which, eventually, will cause suffering, such as burnout and stress.

In *Nietzsche and Philosophy*, Deleuze stresses, "Life goes beyond the limits that knowledge fixes for it, but thought goes beyond the limits that life fixes for it. Thought ceases to be *ratio*. Life ceases to be reaction . . . life making thought active, thought making life affirmative."[143] The element of thought, he stresses, is the sense and values that are produced as a result of an encounter with the forces of life. You can only think affirmatively in relation to active forces. Therefore, you need to experiment with your experiences to see what values and sense they might open up for. What is a beneficial relation? What is a healthy relation? In other words, you need to take seriously your experiences—the feelings that they generate, such as joy or sadness—and one should not evaluate these from a lucrative and higher position but should do so in order to evaluate the values and sense that we already believe and take for granted. Truth, therefore, is not an element of thought. The elements of thought are *sense* and *value*. You question and challenge your ignorance to use it in a constructive way to move beyond your limitations, such as old habits or patterns of reactions. Thus, to give life a purpose is to allow or acknowledge that life activates thought, which then makes life affirmative.

The various forces that resist death, perhaps to maintain the ongoing process of dying, constitute life. What resists death? Love, such as the love of wisdom. Wisdom is integrated in the way we live. "The different kinds of knowledge are also different ways of living, different modes of existing."[144]

It is due to this openness that we mature. I guess this is why being humble comes with philosophizing. Or, why philosophy shares its practice with art. Both can put you in contact with other modes of existence. "Only literature can give you access to spirit from beyond the grave," as Houllebecq makes a character say in *Submission*.

20

THERE IS A LONG HISTORY OF DEBATE IN PHILOSOPHY about the relationship between subject and object. It should be clear by now that the observer cannot be distinguished from what he or she observes. We become when the dualism between subject and object vanishes into a mixed body, where we can no longer distinguish the one from the other but only notice what it produces. As the Norwegian writer Karl Ove Knausgaard writes in *My Struggle* (part V), "Oh, if only I could write about *them*, no, not write about *them* but make my writing *be* them, then I would be happy. Then I would have peace of mind."

To be *them*, you have to become with them. To be alive, you must become life.

* * * *

The process of how an object gradually dissolves in the mind (or vice versa) can be illustrated through the relationship between five categories called the five aggrega-tes:[145]

1. Bodily and physical form
2. Feelings
3. Perceptions (or recognition)
4. Mental functionings (or formations)
5. Consciousness

The assembly of the five aggregates expresses the for-mation, creation, and destruction of all things. Whatever arises will pass; creation and destruction walk hand in hand. "I make, remake and unmake my concepts along a moving horizon, from an always decentered center, from an always displaced periphery which repeats and differen-tiates them."[146]

The bodily and physical forms include the body with its five senses of sight, hearing, smell, taste, and touch. It also includes our nervous system. The bodily and physi-cal forms are part of what it means to be a human being, although not all human beings have functional senses or nervous systems. The human body is always placed in a physical world that stresses how our bodily activities are responses to the various physical stimuli; for example, do you walk, stop, sit, or lie down? Just imagine how your body posture changes depending on the surface on which you walk: ice versus grass, going down versus up, etc. Similarly, seeing and hearing is something that we do. It is a way of exploring the world around us—for example, turning our bodies.

The rest of the five aggregates refer to mental processes, although we can't separate the mind and body as such.

The second aggregate illustrates how we evaluate what we encounter. However, this evaluation is not conceptual, nor does it refer to transcendent moral categories. The evaluation refers to your feelings, whether pleasant, unpleasant, painful, or neutral. It is based on how a person is affected. Likewise, regarding the third aggregate, when you perceive a sensation, you try to recognize it by naming it, conceptualizing it, and attributing its cause. A person's perception is conditioned by his or her culture, history, and physical and emotional state. Imagine you just got fired from a job that you liked, and while sitting on the metro, commuting back to your home, you see many other commuters returning from work. You see them every day, but today you perceive them differently because your situation has changed. In addition, we often suffer because we don't understand how it all comes together, or we don't perceive what really happens but are colored by our emotional state, culture, or historical background. This is not only something that all people have or will experience, but it is also something seen within the political debate, where many cling to certain opinions.

Becoming with emphasizes that the philosopher attempts to bring into being what does not yet exist. Release the part of the event, which it can't actualize itself. Becoming doesn't have any limit because every time something passes, something else arises. Philosophers, therefore, "bring into being that which does not exist," regardless of how it fits with the dominating ideals and norms of society—norms and ideals that are just another set of delusions.[147] It is important that we become aware of the conditioned patterns that most of us repeat without really paying attention. Otherwise, we can easily reproduce rigid gender stereotypes of women and men that still cause so much suffering in contemporary society because doing so reproduces fictional gender identities. Our recognition is connected with awareness. For example, Bergson showed that two forms of recognition exist: an automatic recognition (what I call here default setting or auto pilot) and an aware recognition. The first kind of recognition is a sensory–motoric perception, whereas awareness also activates a person's memory. Recall that the Pali word *sati* and the Sanskrit word *smrti* are in English translated into mindfulness. The basic meaning of *sati* is memory. Mindfulness prevents you from forgetting, which also emphasizes that the present moment or each instant may be the only thing that exists, but it does so because it vibrates in between what is not yet past and what is yet to come. Actualization may be a better word. To recollect, our memory is a creative process because we have to create the memory anew.

Mindfulness, then, combines both present-moment awareness and remembering. The main idea is that the more aware we are, the more nuanced and rich the storage of our memories is. This is of importance because there can be quite a distance between the virtual and the actual—for example, the memory that we are reactivating and the actual situation actualizing it. For example, when I, as a father, bring my children to school in Spain, I may recall how I was once a schoolboy in Denmark. Our memory can also help facilitate a more beneficial nurturing of how we approach life. Basically, all of us learn from experiences, which emphasize that due to our attention, we constantly become aware that our experiences are not final. They, too, undergo change. This is the reason why some people often become less rigid with age. We experience that things can be done differently and yet still work.

The fourth aggregate addresses the mental functioning that operates as your reaction to your perceptions—for example, sensations, ideas, emotions, memories, fantasies, etc. It is here that we may cultivate a wiser response than just a reaction.

* * * *

Nietzsche spoke about philosophy as an active science where critique is positive and not based on resentment. Such an active approach takes three forms:[148] 1) a symptomatology that treats phenomena as symptoms whose sense must be sought in the forces that produce them—for example, feelings; 2) a typology that interprets these forces from the standpoint of their inherent qualities—for example, active or reactive; 3) a genealogy that attempts to evaluate the origin of the forces from the point of view of their nobility—for example, outlining the will to power or will to create. The point is that any force that affects us, the flux of any passing present moment, is treated as a symptom of a will that wills something. For example, what a feeling wants when it passes through me depends on its quality or motive—what is it trying to tell me, and how can I respond (or act) constructively rather than reacting resentfully?

For Nietzsche, "the will to power" is not a will to want something specific; the will is not goal-oriented. Instead, the power is related to wanting what the will wanted—that is, learning to live with what you encounter. This is becoming with.

Meditation is something both creative and giving. It gives place or room for some of the forces that you encounter, while it lets go of others. Cultivating or fertilizing life is an active destruction of what is unhealthy or a positive critique—a critique of joy, as Nietzsche said. It nurtures some forces but not others. In continuation of this thought, the human being also loses his or her privileged position in life or within the ecosystem. Each one of us is just one life living in between many other forms of life, organic and nonorganic. Due to this, we can raise a positive critique toward those who use mindfulness as a romantic tool that can fix or cure things that are broken, or who refuse to take a critical stand as if sexism or racism could ever be considered acceptable. So, instead of cure, a philosophy can heal.

No one owns his or her life, and for this reason, no one can destroy life as such—it passes through us—but we can all change the conditions for life in a way that makes it impossible to go on living.

The last of the five aggregates is the consciousness that I propose is our relationship with life. When we connect with life, we feel alive: we become aware that we are alive. The five aggregates, as I present them here, illustrate how the conscious mind is not inside us. Rather, it is a process of harmonizing with the world, an achieved integration of its qualities. It is life itself that affects the nature of our conscious experience when consciousness is not *about* something but is something.

It suggests that life is consciousness. This also means that we can only take responsible and sustainable decisions—those that are worth repeating—when we connect with life. The Norwegian philosopher Arne Næss said it beautifully: "The world is always in the making,"[149] emphasizing that we have a role to play.

* * * *

The five aggregates present us with *possible* illustrations of how the mind works. The bodily and physical form, for example, refers to how my body and the world intermingle: 1) Something affects me, and I notice how different feelings may be provoked, such as pleasant, unpleasant, and neutral. 2) More specifically, what happened? Why were these emotions expressed? Through a more thorough sensibility, I may be able to classify my experience; for example, an apple, a book, or a car is what I encountered. 3) All of this activates my mental functioning—for instance, this particular experience provokes or awakens desires, wishes, or tendencies, such as "I think of Newton when I see an apple", "I want to read when I see a book," or "I tend to think of accidents when I see a car." 4) My consciousness refers to me being aware of myself as the one who experiences various feelings, perceptions, and thoughts. 5) I think that the five aggregates are activated due to an encounter between different forces—for example, me and what is not me. Then, the order in which feelings, thoughts, or perceptions take place is random and perhaps not always that clear, especially if our feelings are neutral. Still, if we are participating mindfully in life, it is the process as such that we instantaneously become aware of.

* * * *

Let me discuss an ordinary experience. Imagine you encounter a painting by the artist Francis Bacon. Your body is now having an encounter with the weird bodies on the canvas, which activates the five senses. While viewing the picture, you can feel how your body responds. It provokes certain feelings (i.e., pleasant, unpleasant, or neutral). Or perhaps, just seeing one of Francis Bacon's paintings made you feel unpleasant. The experience may cause you to recall other painters who have affected you.

Perhaps you recall Deleuze's book on the artist Francis Bacon and vibrations (or perhaps you are already conditioned by the philosopher's reading, but then you gradually free yourself from Deleuze and relate to Francis unarmed; maybe the French philosopher didn't capture it all). Gradually, it all begins to make sense. What makes sense? A mixture of the feelings that pass over you and how you perceive and interpret what happens while it happens? While all this is happening, you're aware that it happens. You become worthy of the multiplicity of different times, forces, and multiple connections that this particular experience consists of. This is your bodily and mental *relation* with Bacon. You are connected. If you return to experience his paintings later, you will probably experience something recognizable but also something new since what is repeated is always different.

The five aggregates illustrate how each encounter affects a person. Consciousness is to become aware of all these interchanging relations and freely follow the forces of life that emerge when they intersect.

The underlying claim in a philosophy of mindfulness is that relations precede existence (unlike Jean-Paul Sartre, who famously said that "essence precedes existence"). Thus, ignorance is to believe in a fixed and static essence that we tend to feel attachments toward. Ignorance is rela-

ted to a metaphysic of being. "We can destroy only as crea-
tors"[150] by producing alternatives or by creating a practice
where the process of becoming is not interrupted. A belief
in an unchangeable essence is something to overcome; it
must be destroyed. The idea of an unchangeable essence
hinders you from becoming wise and mature; it breaks the
flow of transformation. Susceptibility and receptivity are
important qualities in this process. You expose your ignorance and accept your vulnerability.

AN AFFIRMATIVE PRACTICE

21

THE MAIN ELEMENT OF A PHILOSOPHY OF MIND-fulness is its affirmative approach to life that consists of four phases: to pay attention, to problematize, to make a sustainable decision, and to transform. This approach, I believe, incorporates the best from philosophy and mindfulness: a love of wisdom related to action, that is, where our actions or responses are based on the wisdom we together have acquired.

The first is to *pay attention*—that is, where you intermingle with what happens, carefully unfolding everything. The second is to *problematize*—that is, to bring decisions out in to the open where no road map exists. These two steps emphasize that knowledge does not refer to a textbook; rather, it functions like, and intermingles with, the world. To know is to get dirt under your nails. You don't become a cook by watching a cooking program on television but by sticking all of your body, mind, and senses into the dough. This hyper-attentiveness, awareness, or mindfulness enhances your power to be affected—affected by life. The first two steps are intimately related because to problematize is neither to position nor oppose. Rather, it is a process of exposing yourself; making yourself vulnerable, gradually acknowledging your failures and successes.

This approach is different from any kind of self-development because you're not developing yourself. Actually, you try to overcome yourself by becoming another. It is not a self-centered process—selflessness.

An affirmative approach, therefore, doesn't follow an objective; rather, it ends all goal setting. To learn is to bring the unconscious out; that is to say, that becoming always takes place as an examination within a certain experience. It's a relational competence. To live a life worth living is never to reach a conclusion; it's not a quiz show; rather, it is to stay patiently with the open questions. It's an inconclusive process that might, at first, appear hard—mainly because we are so trained in objective thinking and resolutions—but it is a part of becoming free.

In continuation, the third element is the *decision-making* that follows the previous steps. Paying attention helps you problematize, which clarifies the possible choices. The point is that by paying careful attention with a curious, critical, and open mind, you're able to create choices that you might not have thought were possible. To problematize and pay attention can help you make sustainable decisions, the kind of decisions you wouldn't mind repeating based on your current knowledge. Making a decision is a way of liberating you, leaving behind what is dying or needing to die in order to cultivate and bring into life something more fruitful. The fourth step is *transformation*, which is related to the main role of philosophy: Knowledge transforms. "Philosophy is the art of forming, inventing, and fabricating concepts... All concepts are connected to problems without which they would have no meaning and which can themselves only be isolated or understood as their solution emerges."[151]

The primary task of philosophy is to confront the illusion that problems are something to be solved by choosing between options A, B, or C. Instead, problems are invented every time we do not know right from wrong. How to go on?

These four elements (i.e., paying attention, problematization, decision-making, and transformation) are not something abstract but take place in a concrete and complex life condition. "We are dealing here with a problem concerning the plurality of subjects, their relationships, and their reciprocal presentation."[152]

A possible better world exists as something real but

not yet actualized. The challenge is to intermingle or negotiate with the various forces of life, see what they can be and what they open for, and then create a language in which the will to become can manifest itself.

To problematize, pay attention, decide, and transform. It is not a four-step launch because, at least, the process of problematizing demands your awareness and vice versa. Sometimes, the way we problematize, we become conscious about other aspects. New possibilities emerge and perhaps what we thought was problematic has dissolved by looking more thoroughly.

* * * *

An affirmative approach to life also minimizes the shame of being alive. Sartre developed the idea of shame as being without the possibility to become—that is to say, grow or enhance your capability to act. He writes, "Shame reveals to me that I *am* this being, not in the mode of 'was' or of 'having to be' but in itself."[153] The shame is linked with seeing yourself as a thing, an object, and a tool without the freedom to become. Shame is often combined with dishonor. For example, you can act in a way that you lose your honor, if you believe in a certain moral codex; yet, you can also feel ashamed if you don't try to match what is taking place in your life. The latter is the one I am referring to—not trying to make your own choices. Similarly, you can feel ashamed by making a decision based on negative motives as if you couldn't afford to do otherwise. An example could be group pressure, the need to belong, or pressure from stakeholders. Here, the shame emerges from acting like you're not free. You're being reduced to an instrument. It's saying, "I had no choice."

All decisions in life, of course, are relative. What matters is the level of compromise that you are willing to make (or forced to make). Certain things matter more. Joining a party that you don't fancy may not be as crucial as being in a relationship, whether personal or professional, that makes you more sad than joyous. The evaluation of your life takes place from within—not in light of certain ideals. Therefore, the choices we make refer to modes of existence—not whether you prefer chocolate or strawberry ice cream. It is not a spontaneous maneuver to reorganize your life but is based on careful scrutiny. It's a mindful and careful problematization of your relationship with life.

"We have opposed knowledge to life in order to judge life, in order to make it something blameworthy, responsible or erroneous."[154] When you blame your decision-making on something else (i.e., X made me do it), you appear to have been acting even though no one, including yourself, actually did act. You were just blindly following norms without considering their relevance in this specific situation. Accordingly, when we feel shame or sadness, we should not judge ourselves but evaluate our behavior to understand why we deserve these feelings or thoughts. It emphasizes the immanent norm of doing only what you would like to repeat. If you don't want to be a disloyal friend, unfaithful partner, uninvolved father or citizen, then act accordingly. And if we don't, we will often experience shame or sadness contrary to feeling honest and joyous.

A philosophy of mindfulness is active and socially engaged. You are also participating in a social setting. This is also why to affirm is creative practice, but it must also be created, as affirming difference, as being difference itself. Life is difference. In other words: say yes to life. Therefore, it is not the negative that is the motor. Furthermore, when life is difference, there is not one way that life is supposed to go; evolution is not a process with a specific end goal. We often measure our successes and failures against what we think we should achieve (or expect to achieve). Yet, there is no clear trajectory in life. Your approach to life matters. For example, an open attitude means that you don't wear certain ideas or norms like an impenetrable raincoat. You're flexible, not bendable or being manipulated. You create spaciousness for that which is in the midst of becoming something else. As if it is a dance, you step aside to follow the rhythm of the music but also to give your partner room for his or her movements. You become aware of your surroundings, and they relate and form you.

Thus, you always problematize in the sense of questioning; hereby, you are also aware of what is different or divergent from your expectations. Finally, you become *with* this difference, affirming that life is creative evolution.

* * * *

I have suggested that mindfulness is a process of becoming *with* reality. In doing so, I bring becoming closer to the concept of non-doing. For example, meditation is a form of negativity that breaks with the dominating urge to perform in today's society; non-doing is seeking nothingness or emptiness as a way of liberation from all these performance demands and ideals. Nothingness, as I use it here, doesn't refer to the myth that meditation is about emptying the mind, but rather that nothing is on the agenda except for what passes. Non-doing is becoming with whatever happens, allowing your body and mind to be filled by life, not something useful or good according to certain ideals. Non-doing resembles Melville's "I prefer not to," which some philosophers believe to be a sufficient critique of capitalism. It's an effective critique, as Melville's story illustrates, but it may also be seen as a goody-goody position that, in the long run, is too passive to create substantial changes. Non-doing is one part of freedom—that is, resisting or standing against. Yet, freedom is also to create or invent new ways where we can live out or act. Freedom is being rebellious or against but also becoming something else.

Becoming, then, is a manner of living that is alive. The spiritual and physical, the mind and the body, cohere. For example, every cell in the world contains DNA—animal, vegetal, or bacterial. DNA is the molecule that carries the generic instructions for growth, development, and reproduction of all living organisms. It is "the informational molecule of life, and its very essence consists in being *both single and double*," both being and becoming.[155] Thus, becoming is not only repairing what is broken—that is, reproducing the same (imitation). Rather, an ongoing negotiation takes place as a passage from unconscious to conscious, from being impotent to being empowered. The experience turns experimental until a direction is proposed. "DNA is a *master of transformation*."

Thus, what I propose is that we understand "becoming with" or "becoming other" as something concrete—as a way of living. Deleuze writes, "If it [body] encounters the animal, if it becomes *animalized*, it is not by outlining a form, but on the contrary by imposing through its clarity and nonorganized precision, a zone of where forms become indiscernible."[156] It is where "I," as the one who experiences, and "I," as the one who is being experienced—that is, formed by the outside—become indistinguishable. You are being flexible, not according to an objective as in management, but according to what life faces you with, or what life throws at you. Everything is temporary and provincial. "It is also attests to a high *spirituality*, since what leads it to seek the elementary forces beyond the organic is spiritual will. But this spirituality is a spirituality of the body."[157]

Each encounter with life releases the present living moment beneath and beyond representation. There are no boundaries for life to respect other than what enhances life. This is why paying attention of how certain social settings and structures may affect us, can improve our level of self-awareness. How can we enhance our power to act?

I am imprinted, marked, even transformed by life based on how susceptible I am (i.e., not seduced). Sensation, therefore, is not the same as perceiving because we typically perceive through identification—that is, looking for the same, the known, and the comfortable. Sensation is difference. Becoming deals with intensity, tension, suspense, and excitement—to experience life as movement while it moves you.

Our relationship with life is evaluated beyond a fixed set of norms; "only the subject that incarnated [a life] in the midst of things made it good or bad."[158]

The strongest aspects of such practice are humility, precision, and care. Although we all have to accept that we can't save the world—at least not alone—still we can be part of it and move it in a beneficial direction, for example, one of equality as we care for it, this is a way of passing on the force of life to future generations. We examine our possibilities by paying attention, carefully evaluating what to pass on. It's a generous ethic. We pass on what is sustainable by affirming what is alive.

WHAT ARE YOU CAPABLE OF BECOMING?

22

THE UNDERLYING PREMISE FOR AN AFFIRMATIVE philosophy is freedom. You're not born free; it is something you become through engaging with life in an open and non-normative way. An affirmative philosopher is *free from* interpreting what happens within a certain frame or referent. This requires courage, as well as imagination—not imagination in the sense that you invent things; instead, you're also *free to* invent a plane where what is in the midst of coming into being can flourish. Freedom encourages us to live on the frontiers of our knowledge, gently acknowledge our ignorance and insecurity, yet never resign or fall back to ideals that don't really serve us.

An affirmative philosophy is an invitation to become with life, instead of being obsessed with checks and monetary balances, forced to develop yourself in a certain image, and performing according to predefined ideals, norms, and other marks of prestige and status. Instead of achieve, achieve, achieve, an affirmative philosophy transforms into a mindful plea for non-doing as a way of being worthy to grasp what is actually happening. It's for this reason that freedom is mandatory. It actively cultivates the conditions of reality and invents a more spacious reality that is full of new life forms.

Before we can know what is hindering life from its inherent movement, and before we know what is emerging, we must try to pay attention to what takes place. The process of paying attention can't be stopped, for example, to see if you're on the right track to a desired objective or whether what happens suits a certain moral category. Every time we try to evaluate from another position, we step out of the process, and the process turns into an action. That is the flow of life is turned into a mark in time instead of being with what is in the midst of becoming.

Furthermore, perhaps on a more reflective level, awareness also means that you're aware of how you are affected, as well as the effect you're having. You are aware of where you are. It basically stresses how difficult it can be to encounter what happens when we are unarmed without our expectations, without being under the spell of stereotypes, clichés, group pressure, social norms, and the seductive fantasies of ideologies. We experience life while experimenting with it so that we can actualize a direction that favors life. Nothing else.

All encounters—at least potentially—produce new values. This is the wisdom we have inherited from Nietzsche's saying that God is dead. This death has provided us with the opportunity to leave all transcendent hypotheses behind in favor of a will to examine what may be possible. The death of God is also the death of the self.

Will what we can while exploring what we might be capable of. This requires that we experience, experiment, and evolve in new ways. We move forward with no compass, listening with an open mind and body. Living a life worth living is constituted by all the forces that affect us, but mainly those that resist death by staying in the flux of life. Another way of saying this is to ask: What resists death?

* * * *

Love is the answer. As Roberto Bolaño writes in *Amulet*, "Nothing good ever comes of love. What comes of love is always something better." Love makes life more intense; it is love that makes life go on. It's a gift from life. All we have to do to experience love is to become free.

Life is *not* ruled by the strongest, as in the survival of the strongest, but rather by those who, despite how troubled the world is, are still capable of letting love rule it. Compassion and care is what makes life flourish. To love is to be open and curious . . . to pay attention; it's pure awareness—connections.

To understand is to love. Perhaps this is also why Bolaño emphasized that reading is more important than writing. To read is a way of training not only our concentration but also our empathic capacity to understand other forms of life and how they think, feel, and view things. Only when we understand do we feel compassion, and only then do we know that we need to take care of other forms of life for them to go on living, just like a book will go on living as long as someone is reading it or discussing its metaphors, thoughts, reflections, language, and so forth. Reading is a mindful activity; or at least, if we understand reading as something else, or something more than just consumption, entertainment, or input toward achieving a performance goal, not even as interpretation, but as a way of being transformed by the encounter you are having with the book, then reading can expose you, and so can mindfulness. Unfortunately, it seems like people prefer to communicate rather than read. Let go of ideals, habits, and boundaries to notice the movement of life.

Art initiates a critical—in a positive and joyous sense—investigation of your life with life. Mindfulness has the capacity to do something similar. There, a philosophy of mindfulness is turned inward, as well as outward.

To live your life on purpose is to embed a will to being formed by what frees life, such as generosity, love, and compassion. An affirmative and mindful philosophy is about nurturing a caring and sustainable relationship with life as a way of exploring what may also be possible. Bring into life what is worth repeating—that is, what is in the process of being born.

It is not a matter of judging life in the name of a higher authority, which would be the good, the true, the just, and the beautiful. Nothing is given per se; nothing remains the same in all eternity. Instead of judging, we evaluate every being, action, and passion and even every value in relation to the life they implicate. It is affect as immanent evaluation instead of judgment as transcendent value. It's a more direct and unsophisticated approach saying: "I love" or "I hate" instead of "I judge."[159]

* * * *

Becoming alive begins with paying careful attention. Simone Weil describes it beautifully when she says that attention "consists of suspending our thought, leaving it detached, empty and ready to be penetrated by the object."

Then she adds, that attention is " . . . not seeking anything, but ready to receive in its naked truth the object which is to penetrate it"[160]—ready to receive life.

Thus, which life is worth living?

A life worth living is one where you're alive, penetrated by life. Becoming alive is a never-ending process of problematization; why, how, and what can I become without violating life. A philosophy of mindfulness is being aware that how we learn and how we expect and perceive the world often hinder the free flow of life. It is to actively remove and break down all the screens that keep life imprisoned.

The art of living is becoming better at living without knowing what is the right thing to do *before* you experience it. Therefore, it is not about who you are. It's not about you. Instead, you care about what you are capable of becoming. Life is taking you elsewhere, moving from everywhere to nowhere. Experience becomes us. That is, what you experience, you become.

What are you capable of becoming?

The right thing to do is to live a life worth living, which is to live as much as possible. Now we know what it requires. Nothing comes for free. To be alive, we must become life, because becoming life is being alive.

It is time to connect with life without a filter.

Bibliography

Agamben, G. (1998). *The Coming Community*. Translated by M. Hardt. University of MinnesotaPress.

Amaro, A. (2015). A Holistic Mindfulness. *Mindfulness, Volume 6, issue 1.*

Aristotle (2004). *The Nicomachean Ethics*. Translated by A.K. Thompson, revised with notes and appendices by H. Tredennick. Penguin Books.

Batchelor, S. (1998). *Buddhism Without Beliefs. A Contemporary Guide to Awakening.* Bloomsbury Publishing.

Blanchot, M. (1995). *The Writing of the Disaster.* Translated by Ann Smock. University of Nebraska Press.

Blanchot, M. (1997). *Awaiting oblivion.* Translated by J. Gregg. University of Nebraska Press.

Bogue, R. (2007). *Deleuze's Ways: Essays in Transverse Ethics and Aesthetics.* Routledge.

Braidotti, R. (2011). *Nomadic Theory. The Portable Rosi Braidotti.* Columbia University Press.

Bryant, L. R (2011). "The Ethics of the Event: Deleuze and Ethics without Αρχη." In *Deleuze and Ethics*, ed. by N. Jun & D.W. Smith. Edinburgh University Press.

Buchanan, I. (2000). *Deleuzism. A Metacommentary.* Edinburgh University Press.

Buchanan, I. M. (2011). "Desire and Ethics", *Deleuze Studies,* vol. 5, no. Supplement, pp. 7-20.

Carette, J. and King, R. (2004). *Selling Spirituality: The Silent Takeover of Religion.* Routledge.

Chakrabarty, B. (2014). *Non-Violence. Challenges and Prospects.* Oxford University Press.

Colebrook, C. (2000). "Is Sexual Difference a Problem?" In I. Buchanan and C. Colebrook, eds. *Deleuze and Feminist Theory.* Edingburg University Press.

D'Ors, P. (2012). *Biografia del silencio. Breve ensayo sobre meditación.* Siruela.

Deleuze, G. (1998). *Spinoza: Practical Philosophy.* Translated by R. Hurlye. City Lights Books.

Deleuze, G (1991). *Empiricism and Subjectivity. An Essay on Hume's Theory of Human Nature.* Translated and with introduction by Constantin V. Boundas. Columbia University Press.

Deleuze, G. (1992). *Expressionism in Philosophy: Spinoza.* Translated by Martin Joughin. Zone Books.

Deleuze, G. (1994). *Difference and Repetition.* Translated by Paul Patton. Columbia University Press.

Deleuze, G. (1995). *Negotiations*. Translated by M. Joughin. Columbia University Press.

Deleuze, G. (1996). *Essays Critical and Clinical*. Translated by D.W. Smith and M.A. Greco. Verso.

Deleuze, G. (2000), *Cinema 2. The Time-Image*. Translated by H. Tomlinson and R. Galeta. The Athlone Press

Deleuze, G. (2002a). *Bergsonism*. Translated by H. Tomlinson and B. Habberjam. Zone Books.

Deleuze, G. (2002b). *Nietzsche and Philosophy*. Trans. by H. Tomlinson. Continuum.

Deleuze, G. (2003). *Francis Bacon: The Logic of Sensation*. Translated by Daniel W. Smith. Continuum.

Deleuze, G. (2004). *The Logic of Sense*. Translated by Mark Lester with Charles Stivale. Continuum.

Deleuze, G. (2005). *Pure Immanence: Essays on a Life*. Translated by A. Boyman. Zone Books.

Deleuze, G. & Guattari, F. (1994). *What Is Philosophy?* Trans. by H. Tomlinson and G. Burchell. Columbia University Press.

Deleuze, G. & Guattari, F. (2000a). *Anti-Oedipus. Capitalism and Schizophrenia*. Trans. By R. Hurley, M. Seem, & H. R. Lane. The Athlone Press.

Deleuze, G. & Guattari, F. (2000b). *A Thousand Plateaus. Capitalism and Schizophrenia.* Translation and foreword by Brian Massumi. University of Minnesota Press.

Deleuze, G. & Parnet, C. (2007). *Dialogues II.* Translated by Hugh Tomlinson and Barbara Habberjam. Columbia University Press.

Gethin (1998). *The Foundations of Buddhism.* Shambhala Classics.

Goldstein, J. (2003). *Insight Meditation. The Practice of Freedom.* Shambhala Classics.

Goldstein, J. (2013). *Mindfulness. A Practical Guide to Awakening.* Sounds True.

Gunaratana, B.H. (2014). *Mindfulness in Plain English.* Wisdom Publications.

Hadot, P. (2006). *Philosophy as a Way of Life.* Edited with an introduction by Arnold I. Davidson. Translated by Michael Chase. Blackwell Publishing.

Hahn, N.,H. (2008). *The Miracle of Mindfulness.* Rider Books.

Harvey, P. (2016). Dukkha, Non-Self, and the Teaching on the Four "Noble Truths." In, *A Companion to Buddhist Philosophy*, edited by Steven M. Emmanuel. Wiley Blackwell.

Heaton, J.M. (2014). *Wittgenstein and Psychotherapy*. Palgrave Macmillan.

Heidegger, M. (1969). *Identity and Difference*. Translated and with Introduction by Joan Stambuch. Harper & Row, Publishers.

Kabat-Zinn, J. (2013). *Full Catastrophe Living. How to cope with stress, pain and illness using mindfulness meditation*. Piatkus.

Kabat-Zinn, J. (2014). *Wherever You Go, There You Are. Mindfulness Meditation for Everyday Life*. Piatkus.

Kierkegaard, S. (1991). *Kjerlighedens Gjerninger*. Samlede værker bind 12. Gyldendals Bogklubber.

Kornfield, J. (2002). *A Path With Heart. The Classical Guide Through the Perils and Promises of Spiritual Life*. Rider Books.

Ligotti, T. (2010). *The Conspiracy against the Human Race*. Hippocampus Press.

Lopez, D., S. (2012). *The Scientific Buddha. His Short and Happy Life*. Yale University Press

Massumi, B. (1992). *A User's guide to Capitalism and Schizophrenia*. A Swerve Edition, The MIT Press.

Merleau-Ponty, M. (1962). *Phenomenology of Perception.* Translated C. Smith. Routledge.

Narby, J. (1999). *The Cosmic Serpent. DNA and the Origins of Knowledge.*

Nietzsche, F. (1973). *Will to power.* Translated by W. Kaufmann and R. J. Hollingdale. Random House.

Nietzsche, F. (1974). *The Gay Science.* Translated by W. Kaufman. Vintage.

Nietzsche, F. (2010). *Moralens oprindelse.* Trans. to Danish by N. Henningsen. Det lille forlag.

Næss, A. (1989). *Ecology, community and lifestyle.* Translated by David Rothenberg. Cambridge University Press.

Næss, A. (2002). *Life's Philosophy. Reason and feeling in a Deeper World* (with Per Ingvar Haukeland). Translated by Ronald Huntford. The University of Georgia Press.

Pearson, K.A. (2001). "Pure reserve. Deleuze, philosophy, and immanence". In *Deleuze and Religion,* edited by Mary Bryden, Routledge.

Pearson, K.A. (2014). "Affirmative Naturalism: Deleuze and Epicureanism." In *Cosmos and History: The Journal of Natural and Social Philosophy, vol. 10, no. 2.*

Perloof, M. (1999). *Wittgenstien's Ladder: Poetic Language and the Strangeness of the Ordinary*. University of Chicago Press.

Rahula, W. (1997). *What the Buddha Taught*. Oneworld Publications.

Rimbaud, A. (2003). *Rimbaud Complete, Volume 1: Poetry and Prose*. Translated by Wyatt Mason. Modern Library Paperback Edition.

Rorty, R. (2005). *Philosophy and the Mirror of Nature*. Princeton University Press.

Rosa, H. (2015). *Social Acceleration. A New Theory of Modernity*. Translated by Jonathan Trejo-Mathys. Columbia University Press.

Sartre, J-P. (2003). *Being and Nothingness. An essay on phenomenological ontology*. Translated by Hazel E. Barnes. Routledge.

Schopenhauer, A. (2004). *Essays and Aphorisms*. Selected and translated with an introduction by R.J. Hollingdale. Penguin Books.

Serres, M. (1982). *Hermes. Literature, Science, Philosophy*. Edited by Josué V. Harari and David F. Bell. The John Hopkins University Press.

Serres, M. (1997). *The Troubadour of Knowledge*. Translated by
S. F. Glaser with W. Paulson. The University of
Michigan Press.

Shaw, S. (2014). *The Spirit of Buddhist Meditation*. Yale
University Press.

Smith, D. W. (2011). Deleuze and the Question of Desire:
Towards an Immanent Theory Ethics. In *Deleuze and
Ethics*, edited by D. W. Smith and N. Jun. Edinburgh
University Press.

Stahl, B. & Goldstein, E. (2010). *A Mindfulness-Based Stress
Reduction Workbook*. New Harbinger.

Villani, A. (2007). Responses to a Series of Questions. *Collapse.
Philosophical Research and Development*, Vol. III.Weil,
S. (2005). *Simone Weil. An Anthology*. Edited and
introduced by Sian Miles. Penguin Books.

Wallace, J.D. (2009). *Norms and Practices*. Cornell University
Press.

Weil, S. (2005). *Simone Weil. An Anthology*. Edited and
introduced by Siân Miles. Penguin Books.

Williams, T. T. (2001). *Refuge. An Unnatural History of Family
and Place*. Vintage Books.

Williams, T. T. (2009). *Finding Beauty in a Broken World*.

Vintage Books.

Williams, J. (2012). *Gilles Deleuze's Philosophy of Time. A Critical Introduction and Guide*. Edinburgh University Press.

Williams, J. Mark G. and Kabat-Zinn, Jon (2011). Mindfulness: diverse perspectives on its meaning, origins, and multiple applications at the intersection of science and dharma, *Contemporary Buddhism,* 12: 1, 1-18.

Wittgenstein, L. (2009). *Philosophical Investigations.* Trans. by G. E. M. Anscobe, P. M .S. Hacker, & J. Schutle. Wiley Blackwell.

Wilson, J. (2014). *Mindful America. The Mutual Transformation of Buddhist Meditation Meditation and American Culture.* Oxford University Press.

Endnotes

1   Bogue, 2007, p. 7.

2   Bryant, 2011, p. 29. Furthermore, Buchanan, 2011, p. 7, said, 'that it is difficult if not impossible to answer the question "what is the right thing to do?" from a Deleuzian perspective.' This book is an attempt to overcome this question, not necessarily answer it.

3   Foucault in Deleuze and Guattari, 2000a, p. xiii.

4   Hadot 2006, p. 83. Furthermore, Pearson, 2014, p. 122, writes: "… he [Deleuze's] tells us, 'life' is not simply an idea or matter of theory but concerns a way of being, a style of life, and a manner of living. For Deleuze, if philosophy has a use it is to be found in the doctrine of Epicureans, as well as in later thinkers such as Spinoza and Nietzsche, namely, the creation of the free human being and an empirical education in the art of living well. An empirical education in the art of living requires, among other things, questioning how life works, not what it means (as if meaning was already given)."

5   Wittgenstein in a letter to his friend Normal Malcolm, here quoted from Perloof, 1999, p. 178.

6   Respectively: Kabat-Zinn, 2014, p. 4; Stahl & Goldstein, 2010, p. 15; Rahula, 1997, p. 73.

7   Weil, 2005, p. 233.

8   Deleuze, 1994, p. xxi.

9   Deleuze, 2007, p. 90; Deleuze, 2004, p. 285.

10   Kabat-Zinn, 2013 p. 200 and 217.

11   Pearson, 2001, p. 141.

12   Shaw, 2014, p. 32

13   Deleuze, 2002b, p. 4.

14   Deleuze, 2006, p. 360.

15   Deleuze & Guattari, 1994, p. 43.

16   Deleuze & Guattari, 1994, p. 92. Elsewhere, Deleuze, 1994, p. 58 writes, "the oneness and identical self, and God is retained so long as the self is preserved." According to Smith, 2012, p. 81, "Nietzsche had already seen that the death of God becomes effective only with the death of the self." Metaphysic of becoming is the "death" of metaphysic of being with its attachment to various forms of institutionalized fictionalizations fixations: norms, ideals, and the self as something unchangeable.

17   Deleuze and Guattari (1994, 171)

18   Deleuze, 1995, p. 143

19   Deleuze, 1996, p. 4.

20   Deleuze, 2002b, p.185. Italics in original.

21   Deleuze, 1995, p. 133.

22   Ortega y Gasset, 1972, p. 42.

23   Deleuze, 1991: "relations are always external to their terms", p. x, 66, 99 and 101. Everything begins in the middle; the outside forms us.

24   Deleuze and Guattari, 1994, p. 109.

25   Villani, 2007, p. 41.

26   Deleuze, 2000, p 146-7; Deleuze, 1994, 154

27   Heidegger, 1969, p. 54.

28   Wittgenstein, 2001, p. 89.

29   Smith, 2012, p. 274.

30   Deleuze and Guttari, 1994, 100

31   Bloch quoted from Buchanan, 2000, p. 117.

32   Deleuze and Guattari 1994, p. 100; see also Deleuze 1994, p. xx.

33   Williams, J., 2012, p. 8 and 9.

34   Serres, 1982, p. 72.

35   Deleuze and Guattari, 1994, p. 100.

36   Deleuze and Guattari, 1994, p. 158. They go on to write: "Each component of the event is *articulated or effectuated* in
an instant, and the event in the time that passes between these
instants; but nothing happens within *the virtuality* that has only
meanwhiles as components and an event as composite becoming. Nothing happens there, but everything becomes, so that the
event has the privilege of beginning again when time is past.
Nothing happens, and yet everything changes, because becoming continues to pass through its components again to restore
the event that is actualized elsewhere, at a different moment.
When time passes and takes the instant away, there is always a
meanwhile to restore the event. It is a *concept* that apprehends
the event, its becoming, its inseparable variations; whereas a
function grasp a state of affairs, a time and variables, with their
relations depending on time."

37   Deleuze, 2005, p. 27. For the term 'immanent ethics'
see Smith, 2012.

38   Deleuze, 2002b, p. 1–2.

39   Deleuze, 2002b, p. 9

40   Deleuze, 2002b, p. 97.

41   Nietzsche, 1974, p. 274

42   Deleuze, 2002b, p. 68. Italics in original; see also
Deleuze, 1994, p. 7.

43   Deleuze, 2004, p. 169.

44   Serres, 1997, p. 167

45   Deleuze, 2004, p. 170.

46   Serres, 1997, p. 167

47   From the *Manual* of Epictus, but here quoted from Hadot, 2006, p. 136.

48   Deleuze, 1988, p. 125

49   Deleuze & Guattari, 2000b, p. 3.

50   Braidotti, 2011, p. 167.

51   Deleuze & Guattari, 1994, p. 82.

52   From the documentary film *Müdigkeitsgesellschaft–Byung-Chul Han in Seoul/Berlin* directed by Isabella Greeser.

53   Han 2011, in the interview "The Terror of Positivity" by Vera Tollmann in *Springerin*.

54   Trejo-Mathys, 2013, p. xxiv (Translator's Introduction)

55   Rosa, 2015, p. xxxviii.

56   Deleuze, 2004, p. 61.

57   Wallace, 2009, p. 19.

58   Blanchot, 1997, p. 21.

59   Williams and Kabat-Zinn, 2011, p. 1.

60   Braidotti, 2011, p. 119.

61   Pearson 1997, p. 109.

62   Deleuze, 2000, p. 172.

63   Deleuze, 2000, p. 173 & 171.

64   Deleuze, 2000, p. 172.

65   Williams, 2008, p. 29. The flowing quotes are on p. 29, 34, 39, 71, and 88.

66   Woolf quoted from Deleuze & Guattari, 2000b, p. 263.

67   Deleuze & Guattari, 2000b, p. 25.

68   Deleuze & Guattari, 1994, p. 181.

69   Deleuze & Guattari, 2000a, p. 1.

70   Goldstein, 2013, p. 281-82.

71   Goldstein, 2013, p. 281-82.

72   Blanchot, 1995, p. 26-28.

73   Gethin, 1998, p. 2.

74   Shaw, 2014, p. 9.

75   Deleuze & Guattari, 2000b, p. 20 & 8.

76   Wittgenstein, 2009, §124.

77   Batchelor, 1998, p. 1. See also Wilson, 2014, p. 15-16 for an interesting and critically analysis of how mindfulness entered the American mainstream.

78   Goldstein, 2003, p. 3.

79   Braidotti, 2011, p. 153.

80   Braidotti, 2011, p. 153.

81   Chakrabarty, 2014, p. xxiv. Næss, 1989, links nonviolence with interconnection and Self-realisation (closely related with becoming as I use it here, where Self-realisation is not egoism). The point is that through a wider and more flexible "self" every living being is intimately connected. And it's exactly due to this connectivity that practice of nonviolence is obvious. Nonviolence puts emphasis on the equal right to live for all human beings as well as non-humans.

82   Amaro, 2015, p. 64. See also Harvey, 2016, p. 26. Harvey mentions that "noble Truth" may be better translated as "true reality" as in 'the First True Reality,' furthermore he prefers to translate dukkha with pain, not suffering.

83   Ligotti, 2010, p. 130 & 28.

84   Williams, 2001, p. 52. This resembles what the Buddha said, "Both in the past and now, I set forth just this: *dukkha* and the cessation of *dukkha*", quoted from Harvey (2016, 26).

85   Smith, 2012, p. 149.

86   Wittgenstein in *Philosophical Occasions 1912-1951*, but quoted from Heaton, 2014, p. 7.

87   Gethin, p. 81. Gethin talks about the "right action" instead of as I of the "balanced". The Pati word *sammá* can be translated as upright, balanced, or attuned; in other words, it is not "right" as in opposition to wrong, see Amaro, 2015.

88   Shaw, 2013, p. 24.

89   Kornfield, 2002, p. 311.

90   Gethin, 1998, p. 84.

91   Goldstein, 2003, p. 15.

92   Shaw, 2013, p. 223

93   Lopez, 2012, p. 74.

94   Rorty, 2005, p. 10.

95   Deleuze, 2006, p. 31.

96   Gethin, 1998, p. 215.

97   Kabat-Zinn, 2014, p. 24.

98   Kornfield, 2002, p. 147.

99   Gethin, 1998, p. 216.

100   Goldstein, 2003, p. 124

101   Goldstein, 2003, p. 127

102   Kornfield, 2002, p. 280.

103   Braidotti, 2011, p. 164.

104   Kierkegaard, 1991, p. 211. My translation. The whole idea of building anything presupposes love.

105   "Thus mindfulness is at the same time a means and an end, the seed and the fruit. When we practice mindfulness in order to build up concentration, mindfulness is seed. But mindfulness itself is the life of awareness: the presence of mindfulness means the presence of life, and therefore mindfulness is also the fruit. Mindfulness frees us of forgetfulness and dispersion and makes it possible to live fully each minute of life. Mindfulness enables us to live," Hahn, 2008, p. 14.

106   Kabat-Zinn, 2013, p. xxxv. In addition, Goldstein, 2013, p. 13, writes that mindfulness "makes any spiritual path possible. Mindfulness has several meanings and functions, all of which are key to the growth of wisdom."

107   Carette and King, 2004, p. 170 where the authors speak about two stages of privatization: "first, individualization, through a process of psycho-political normalization, and second, corporatization, through the process of neoliberalism." The result is that much spirituality serves as a tool for consumerism and capitalism. A tendency that tragically makes more people suffer and therefore likely to be future consumers of the next "quick fix healing."

108   Gunaratana, 2014, p. 131ff. The translation of the Pali word "sati" was not always mindfulness; other terms were "watchfulness," "well awake," "correct memory", and so forth.

109   Gunaratana, 2014, p. 131ff.

110   Deleuze, 2007, p. 50.

111   Goldstein, 2003, p. 118

112   Goldstein, 2003, p. 118.

113   For example, Amaro, 2015, and Lopez, 2012.

114   Colebrook, 2000, p. 87

115   D'Ors, 2012, p 43. My translation from Spanish.

116   Deleuze and Guattari, 1994, p. 6.

117   Deleuze and Guattari, 1994, p. 28.

118   Schopenhauer, 2004, p. 43.

119   Aristotle, 2004, p. 23 (1109b).

120   Kabat-Zinn, 2014, p. 4

121   Agamben, 1998, p. 1.

122   Serres, 1997, p. 8.

123   Rimbaud, 2003, p. 365. Later he writes (p. 367), "I mean that you have to be a *seer*, mold oneself into a *seer*."

124   Kabat-Zinn, 2014, p. 44 & 45.

125   Kabat-Zinn, 2013, p. 6

126   Deleuze, 1992, p. 254

127   Merleau-Ponty, 1962, p. 39.

128   Rimbaud, 2003, p. 195

129   Hanh, 2008, p. 11.

130   Purser, 2014, p. 685. On p. 683, he writes, "In many respects, 'being in the present moment' has become the holy grail of therapeutic mindfulness." The risk is that the present moment becomes an object of meditation.

131   Braidotti, 2011, p. 35.

132   Deleuze, 2003, p. 46.

133   Deleuze, 1992, p. 383.

134   Purser (2015)

135   Lopez, 2012, p. 109.

136   Deleuze & Guattari, 2000b, p. 206.

137   Deleuze, 1992, p. 256.

138   Næss, 2002, p. 15. Deleuze, 1992, p. 258, writes, "All a body can do (its power) is also its 'natural right'… Everyone seeks, soul and body, what is useful or good for them." In other words, it is our human right to relate in a favorable way to what we encounter. "Thus affections at each moment determine *conatus*, but *conatus* is at each moment a seeking of what is useful in terms of the affections that determine it. Whence a body always goes as far as it can, in passion as in action, and what a body can do is its right."

139   Deleuze, 1992, p. 230.

140   Deleuze, 1988, p. 99.

141   Goldstein, 2003, p. 133.

142   Spinoza's *Ethics* here quoted from Deleuze, 1988.

143   Deleuze, 2002b, p. 101.

144   Deleuze, Spinoza, 289

145   Gethin, 1998, p. 135-36.

146   Deleuze, 1994, p. xxi.

147   Deleuze, 1994, p. 147

148   I follow Deleuze's reading, p. 75 cf.

149   Næss, 2002, p. 83.

150   Nietzsche, 1974, p.122.

151   Deleuze and Guattari, 1994, p. 2 & 16.

152   Deleuze and Guattari, 1994, p. 16.

153   Sartre, 1993, p. 351.

154   Deleuze, 2002b, p. 35.

155   Narby, 1999, p. 88, 90 and 92. What I propose is that
the DNA changes when a person incorporates the qualities of
what he or she is becoming; of course, without ever becoming
an actual snake, woman, or anything else. This idea touches
upon Deleuze and Guattari's concepts: molar and molecular.
"Becoming is an equilibrium-seeking system at a crisis point
where it suddenly perceives a derterministic constraint, becomes 'sentitive' to it, and is catapulted into a highly unstable
supermolecular state enveloping a bifurcating future," writes
Massumi, 1992, p. 95. Later he writes, "Becoming is directional
rather than intentional" (p. 95).

156   Deleuze, 2003, p. 46.

157   Deleuze, 2003, p. 47. It continues, "the spirit is the body itself, the body without organs."

158   Deleuze, 2006, p. 288

159   Deleuze, 2000, p. 141. I follow the original closely in my paraphrasing.

160   Weil, 2005, p. 8.

About the author

Finn Janning is a writer and a philosopher. He has studied philosophy, literature and business administration at Copenhagen Business School (CBS), and at Duke University. He earned his PhD in practical philosophy from CBS in 2005.

In the mid nineties, he was introduced to meditation and Buddhist philosophy, yet it was not until 2013 that he began a daily meditation practice. In addition he holds a Master Degree in Mindfulness from the University of Zaragoza (2017).

Janning's work has been featured in *Epiphany, Under the Gum Tree*, and *South 85 Journal*, as well as in several academic journals. His most recent book is *The Happiness of Burnout* (Köenig Books, London, 2015).

He lives in Barcelona, Spain with his wife and their three children.